Contents

Introduction   7

Chapter One   Uplands and Lowlands   10

Chapter Two   Planting Ideas for the Future   22

Chapter Three   Men of Legend   31

Chapter Four   New Horizons   45

Chapter Five   New Faces, New Challenges   56

Chapter Six   Reflections on the Glory Days   65

Chapter Seven   Working in Co-operation   73

Chapter Eight   Time to Realise That Ambition   83

Chapter Nine   Expansion and Development   89

Chapter Ten   The Stony Path to Exports   99

Chapter Eleven   Opportunities   110

Chapter Twelve   The Scourge of Foot and Mouth Disease   116

Chapter Thirteen   The Aftermath   131

Appendix   The rules for registration of Welsh Black cattle,
                   extracted from the 1905 Herd Book   136

Acknowledgements

I dedicate this book to the memory of my uncles and in particular to my Uncle Dick, who taught me most of what I know of Welsh Black Cattle breeding.
I appreciate the tolerance shown by my dear wife Dorothy and my family during the writing of this book.

I also wish to record my appreciation of the valued assistance and advice given by Mrs Moira Smith and Mrs Jean Brown, who typed my original manuscript.

John Rees, Comins Coch, Aberystwyth
May 2003

The author, John Pryse Rees,
aged 10½, August 1940

In Garni's

The autobiography of a well-known breeder

John Rees

First impression: 2003
© Copyright: John Rees and Y Lolfa Cyf., 2003

Cover photograph: Arvid Parry Jones
Thanks to the National Library of Wales for the photograph of Cilgerran on page 28
Design: Ceri Jones

ISBN: 0 86243 688 5

Published and printed in Wales
by Y Lolfa Cyf., Talybont, Ceredigion SY24 5AP
e-mail ylolfa@ylolfa.com
website www.ylolfa.com
tel. (01970) 832 304
fax 832 782
isdn 832 813

In Garni's Wake

The autobiography of a well-known breeder of Welsh Black Cattle

John Rees

dinas

Introduction

Parallel with each other are certain aspects of rural life that affected me in my roles as husband, father, citizen and farmer. The predominant theme of this autobiographical book is the development of Welsh Black cattle over the seventy-plus years of my association with the breed. There have been other impacts, too, in the domestic pattern of life on the farm, as well as the rules and regulations that govern and enforce changes in our way of working, and the ways in which our homes are organised. Since home is where the heart is, I shall give it the importance it deserves, by mentioning the changes on the domestic front that I have seen.

To begin with the Welsh Blacks seems appropriate because of their importance to me, and it might be helpful if I briefly chart their progress from the year 1874, when the first volume of the Herd Book was published, until the present day. There were 96 females and 56 bulls recorded in the first volume of the Herd Book, and the first cow ever entered was ANNIE LAURIE, born in 1859, at Cefnfaes; she turned out to be a multi-prize-winner. For those who wish to find out more, I would refer them to a useful source of statistics and background information. G. Williams Edwards, Secretary of the Society for a time, wrote a booklet entitled *The History of the Society from 1874 to 1962*, in which, in addition to his valuable description of the way the breed became increasingly important, he gives details of the registrations and numbers of Society members over the period he covers, as well as dates, entry figures and prices from the sales. Study of these details indicates the rise and fall in popularity of the sales venues, fluctuations in prices and the changing ratio of cows to bulls.

The Welsh Black has become recognised as the beef breed that can produce milk, although it was first recognised for the quality and quantity of its milk, the beef accolade coming later. The earliest animals were to be found in Wales in pre Roman times, and were believed to have been brought here by the Ancient Britons. They provided the gene pool from which our herds have been bred, although the first cattle would have looked somewhat different from those of today. Their survival through more than 2,000 years is probably due to their adaptability to many types of terrain and their ease of management, as much as to anything else. My association with this breed was, firstly, with the milk, as I shall explain.

Since I was born, in 1930, life on the farm has changed more rapidly than at any time before, not just for the farmer and farm worker, but also for the women. My own wife spent far too much of her youth and energy running our historic farm, Brysgaga, in Bow Street, and now that we live in our retirement bungalow, with every modern convenience, she has time to blossom and enjoy some leisure. Many believe that farm life is idyllic. It was always hard, for the women as well as the men, and my grandmother, mother and wife would have been amongst the first to affirm this.

Many books have been written about the life of the male farm worker over the ages, yet little has been recorded about the life of their womenfolk. For this reason, I shall do no more than make passing mention, as I write, of the work of the men. In 1994, the National Museum of Wales in Cardiff published a booklet, *A Woman's Work: Housework 1890-1960*. The Welsh title is *O'r Gwaith i'r Gwely: Cadw tŷ 1890-1960*. This translates as '*From Work to Bed: Housework 1890-1960*, and summarises the matter very neatly. The Museum made a collection of interviews with housewives and, where available, used contemporary photographs. One daily duty for many women living in the countryside, not only in Wales, right up to and including the early part of the twentieth century, was obtaining a supply of domestic water. Often, it had to be carried some distance, from the nearest well, or from a standpipe, a task that usually fell to the children of the family, who would spend Sunday evening carrying buckets of water home, ready for the Monday wash. The first picture and story in the Museum's booklet shows a Pembrokeshire farm kitchen, circa 1930, and the housewife is doing some washing in a galvanised iron basin, in a kitchen that looks much as it did generations before. The floor consists of rough slabs of stone, the single window is tiny and deep-set, and the whole place reeks of poverty and daily grind, more reminiscent of a cave than a human habitation. There are few cooking pots in evidence, and no food to be seen, although what there was would have been stored in a cool pantry. Without refrigerators and freezers to store fresh food under ideal conditions, meat was salted and used as required, butter and milk would turn rancid in high summer, and fruit and vegetables were only available in season, so that winter rations were short on vitamins and lacked variety and flavour.

Until motor transport became commonplace, the housewife was responsible for baking her bread, preserving fruit and vegetables, making and cleaning clothes, and caring for a larger number of children than is common nowadays, so that she had no rest and no recreation. When she went to market, it was to sell surplus butter, cheese and eggs, rarely to shop for things to carry home. Even mains electricity came late to rural Wales, and it was well after the Second World War when the supply came to Bow Street. When we consider how dependent we are on our regular power supply and the motor vehicles we use daily, it becomes clear what amazing alterations they brought in their wake.

Other duties fell to the rural housewife, she helped to churn for butter; she kept poultry for the eggs which she had to take to market one day a week; the home garden was her responsibility; and she had to keep her home spotless, her only aid being the muscles in her arms and back, and the broom and brush, pail and mop. Small wonder, then, that the Museum said that her lot was work until bed-time. If one thinks, too, of the regular pregnancies, the home-nursing duties and the cost of medical treatment, it was hardly surprising to discover that many country women had skill with herbal remedies, and a profound knowledge of the virtues to be found in the flora and fauna around their homes.

I have mentioned all these things, because they formed the background to my childhood and early adulthood, and help to define who and what I am and once was.

To illustrate how far this hands-on contact with the countryside is slipping away, and on the subject of rules and regulations surrounding and changing present day farming, I should like to tell a little, contemporary, true story, although, for obvious reasons, names are omitted. It happened at a county show, that the Rural Affairs Minister from the Welsh Assembly was walking along the sheep-lines, in company with his local Assembly member. A shepherd, who was with his sheep in the pen behind these two gentlemen, had bent down, to attend to the foot of one animal, and could not be seen, when he overheard the Rural Affairs Minister ask his companion,

'Tell, me, how can you tell the difference between an ewe and a ram?'

No wonder that farmers have such confidence in the expertise of those who formulate farming policy! In the course of this autobiography, I shall have occasion to complain, from time to time, about the sort of changes that have come about, many of which seem detrimental, rather than beneficial, to those engaged in agriculture. The anecdote given above might explain, in part, why some of us feel dejected about the future of our industry. If I were asked to pinpoint one of the most far reaching changes in the agricultural industry, I think it would have to be the way in which food is distributed over long distances to reach the consumer, instead of local farms supplying local needs, and customers being familiar with their suppliers.

CHAPTER ONE
Uplands and Lowlands

Welsh Black cattle, descendants of a breed that was found in Wales in pre-Roman times, have been at the core of my working life since I was a child, when my father ran a Welsh Black milking herd at the farm known as Brysgaga, situated in Bow Street, a few miles north of Aberystwyth, which I continued after his death.

I shall start this book with a brief overview of the way things changed as I was growing up. My parents moved to Brysgaga towards the end of 1930, nine months after I was born, and they found it difficult to make ends meet, due to the general economic depression, which, at that time, affected agriculture as severely as industry and commerce. In my own long experience, I have seen the return of a depression in agriculture, and many once prosperous businesses collapse. In the case of my parents, however, who were not the types to yield to misfortune, they set to and worked hard enough to survive.

My father was a much-travelled individual and had a sharp wit. Before the First World War, he spent some time shepherding sheep out in

Author's father at Brysgaga Farm with some of his sheep dogs, including a Merle

Australia. I remember him saying how a Chinese hairdresser cut his hair and made a poor job of it. The Chinese barber's only comment in response to father's criticism was, 'Ah Well! All same one week.'

While shepherding, one evening, on the bank at Brysgaga, sometime before the days of myxomatosis, when rabbits were plentiful, an amateur poacher was caught trespassing by my father. The man approached him, rather embarrassed, and said, 'Rees, the rabbits won't be many less because of me.'

To which my father, assuming a stern look, replied, 'That's the problem; you are such a bad shot, you might hit one of my cows, or one of my ewes, and kill them.'

Today, on most farms of moderate size, thanks to modern equipment and means of transport, the work is done by one man, with occasional help from neighbours and friends, and the rest of the family is in other employment. Back in my childhood, there were two men and a maid to help with tending the cows and doing general maintenance round the farm, as required. My mother ran a sideline in Bed and Breakfast for holiday-makers, to eke out the family finances, as well as doing her share of farm work.

These were the days when locally produced goods fed local people, and my father had a milk round, as did another four local farmers. If, at the end of the round, there was any surplus milk, this was taken to the local butcher, Evans Bach, Penygarn, who was able to dispose of it. At first, my father went his rounds with a primitive hand cart, but the volume of milk increased as time went by, and in 1933 the Milk Marketing Board was established. This was a co-operative for milk producers and it introduced a new method of distribution. A lorry called every day and picked up the churns of milk from a concrete stand on the side of the road in Cross Street, by my neighbour's farm, Gaerwen. Mr. John Jones of Gaerwen was another milk producer, and he and my family shared this milk stand with two more local producers.

The first Milk Marketing Board factory was at Pontllanio, and Felinfach, by Lampeter, came later on. Although the M. M. B. took the bulk of our milk production, the yield continued to increase and my father decided to sell the surplus locally; for the purpose, he bought himself a pony and a milk cart. Some mornings, when the M. M. B. lorry called for our churns, there was a delay, caused by the pony, who was not always amenable to being caught and harnessed up to the cart. Then, it could take a lot of effort, time and patience to get it between the shafts. The M. M. B. driver was not too happy with our pony, either, especially in winter, when the roads between farms were often covered in ice and snow and his time-table was already in jeopardy. When I had time, I would go on the delivery rounds with my father, and grew familiar with every inch of the Bow Street district.

Shortly after the Second World War, in about 1946/7, electricity came to Bow Street, and it was

Pupils at the old Rhydypennau School, before World War II; 1937

possible for us to use a milking machine, which made life a lot easier and did away with the need to sit on a stool, pulling at a cow's teats, taking an occasional kick, or having a tail swished across one's face and one's cap flung into the cow muck.

For several years thereafter, things continued in much the same way, until the arrival in the 1970s of the pipe-line and the bulk tank. Now, the bulk tanker called daily, the pony was put out to grass and the only sound was the gurgling noise as milk disappeared into the tanker and our own tank was left empty.

During 1978/9 I was enticed to go out of milk production. The Common Market Agricultural Policy was playing havoc with farming in Wales, as it was in the rest of the United Kingdom, and it was a wise man who could foresee where things were leading. I decided that the time had come, along with the right circumstances and sufficient acreage, to realise my ambition and go in for breeding the Welsh Blacks.

There have been many other changes in and around Brysgaga since the day when I first came into the world. Bow Street was expanding by 1939; just before the outbreak of the war the price of a building plot was £20 and the cost of building a substantial house was £500, which seems astonishing when compared with prices today. I am now retired, and my son Rowland is the new incumbent at Brysgaga; his daily routine is vastly different from what my own was, and that of my father.

Though unable to own a herd of pedigree Welsh Blacks until I was into middle life, I was always closely involved with them, firstly through my uncles and then through my friends and neighbours, and had always yearned to have a herd of my own. In retrospect, it is clear that this close association with those who managed the breed must have given me some insight into the animals and their advantages, particularly once the breed began to develop in response to the needs of changing times, so that when I did get started, I was able to produce some cattle I am proud of and to serve the Breed Society to the best of my ability, once as president, and now as chairman of the Council and chairman of the Marketing Steering Committee. Indeed, there has been a close link between the progress of the breed, as the

Welsh Black Society approaches its centenary year, 2004, and my personal life.

****

The origin of the Welsh Black cattle breed goes back into the mists of time, and the subject has been ably researched by Jenny Buckton, whose book should be ready for the Society's centenary. The breed has become famous and something we treasure, and it will continue to improve.

My early experiences with cattle provided the best training any Welsh Black breeder could wish for. I have learnt the value of their hardiness and capacity for milk production as well as their beef qualities, all essential to the success of the breed. It is because of their ability to adapt to a variety of conditions and husbandry systems that the original image of the little, upland brood-cow has been left behind. Welsh Blacks have made enormous strides in response to the use of modern, objective selection techniques and the diffusion of high-performance bloodlines, and have shown themselves comparable in commercial beef-value both to imported and indigenous breeds and to crosses. The Welsh Black has all these attributes, and ease of management, too.

When I was a child there was no electricity, few telephones, and motorised transport was sparse and primitive. In spite of limited travel opportunities, people were not bereft of human company; the effort was made to have contact with members of other households, the occasions for doing so were protracted and often yielded colourful stories about individuals and their proclivities, oft-repeated and none the worse for that. They are the stuff of the times which contributed so much to my life story that I do not hesitate to share them with my readers.

It was definitely the spirit of co-operation that helped the farmers to minimise costs and survive the hard times in farming. To partake in selling stock at Menai Bridge, breeders from Ceredigion and beyond shared a lorry, and on the day before the sale the lorry collected stock from the breeders, who, with their stockmen, stayed the night at the sale venue and the Council members attended a Council meeting, invariably held at the offices of the auctioneers, Pritchards of Bangor. There were few farmers able to afford a car in the thirties and forties. They invariably took advantage of the one car owner in their midst and shared the car with him. He was not always very sure of the route and sometimes they missed their way.

I remember once, when a party of farmers were returning home from Menai Bridge, guided by a vocal stalwart occupying one of the back seats, who constantly reminded them to keep to the sea. This they did. It transpired that they returned home to Ceredigion, having circled round the Lleyn Peninsula, come down the Cambrian Coast and back to Dyfi Bridge. They arrived home at

Author's mother, Uncle Tom and the author himself, taken in 1971 at a 21st birthday party

about midnight. A characteristic of this particular driver was that he was steady on a straight piece of road, but rather sudden when turning the steering wheel at a corner.

I begin with mention of my uncle Tom Jenkins, who was a bachelor, living with my maternal grandmother on an upland farm at the head of the Artists' Valley, so-called because its beauty, the silver birches around the river, and the Einion Falls near Furnace, the village close to Eglwysfach, attracted many landscape painters. Above the village is the Foel Fawr, and the track to Bwlcheinion runs up a steep incline beside the river. Once you reach the top, the view of the Dyfi Estuary is breathtaking. To my childish eyes, the wonder of it was all the greater if, in the far distance and on a very clear day, I could glimpse some of the land at Ynys, which belonged to another of my uncles. Still further up, beyond the valley, is Bwlchymaen, or what remains of it. This was another holding in the possession of our family; vast, bleak, and inhospitable, it is reached by a track which begins in the farmyard at Bwlcheinion. There was one occasion when two ramblers met my uncle in the yard. They admired the view, exclaiming, 'What a lovely aspect.' The farmyard cockerel began treading a hen, and my uncle replied, 'And that's another aspect.'

Uncle Tom had quite a way with words. It was during a stormy, blustery bout of weather with prolonged gale-force winds, when Tom looked up at the sky and said, 'I wish the Almighty would put his finger up her arse, to shut her off.'

There are more stories I could tell about Uncle Tom; there was the one about a ram, that is worth repeating. Tom was up on Bwlchymaen mountain, rounding up sheep for shearing, as he had done many times in the past. There was one ram amongst the flock who had seen it all before and was determined to avoid the humiliation of being penned, hobbled, and shorn by hand, which was a slow and exhausting job for the shepherd, who still sheared by hand in those days, and could be a bit trying for the animals. The artful ram evaded the dogs and the shearers, and scurried off across the mountain. The dogs were too busy with the rest of the flock to give chase, and the ram managed to dodge them for a year or two.

At last, someone thought of a cunning plan by which to beat the ram and get him divested of what had become a truly astonishing coat of wool. It was high summer and the bracken was thick and dense; by moving a large gathering of sheep against him, the ram was driven into the thickest part of the bracken, from which he could not escape in any direction. A young shepherd pounced on him, grabbed him by the horns and led him off to be penned. Not only had the ram evaded the shears, but he had not been dipped either, and it is a fair bet that he felt much better for losing his coat and his parasites.

On the subject of hand-shearing, the old shepherds developed very hard muscles in the hand that used the shears. It was almost a symbol of their craft.

Uncle Tom was friendly with his neighbour, Brigadier General Lewis Pugh, and it was usual for them to meet one another at a sheep fair, held in the autumn at Machynlleth. They noticed a particularly stout gentleman with a large corporation, and my uncle made some comment about him. The Brigadier General smiled and said, 'Aye, the beginning of the end.'

The house at Bwlcheinion and the presence in it of my grandmother remain firmly lodged in my memory. This was no ordinary farmhouse: some of its exterior walls were slated almost to ground level, which gave it an aura of remoteness. And the kitchen at its heart did full justice to the rest of the building. It had a slate-slab floor, a large inglenook fireplace; a huge and magnificent dresser, and there was an enormous table at the centre, in keeping with the fine proportions of the room.

These were special things which I took for granted; but a friend, who visited the farmhouse in later years, told me that the sheer beauty of this interior inspired something approaching awe. To be received by the old lady herself made the long trek up the rough, potholed track seem to my friend to have been a sort of pilgrimage: she was regal.

To me my grandmother always seemed to be old and I could never imagine what she might have been like in her youth. I can, now. She was born and grew up on a farm called Tanllan, on the edge of the Borth Bog; whose homestead stood opposite the church at Llangynfelin, the church attended by my grandmother's family. Perhaps because it was more High Anglican than the closer church at Eglwysfach, this was also the parish church attended by the inhabitants of Glandyfi Castle, Voelas Hall, Cymerau Mansion, and the whole cluster of aristocratic families who were neighbours at that northern edge of the county.

Unlike her sisters, my grandmother was assimilated into this circle. How this happened, I'm not sure. It is possible that there was some personal connection, or it might simply have arisen from her natural distinctiveness. She certainly shared the pastimes of her friends, and continued to do so after her marriage to my grandfather. Her side-saddle, which has come down to me, is beautifully made of the finest leather; and it is clear that she entered into the usual rivalries of the day, in sporting the most elegant carriage and accessories.

My grandfather was also one of these neighbours but although he was a farmer of substance, he was not a member of the aristocracy. He farmed sheep on a very extensive tract of land and seems to have had the means to improve the breeding of his sheep by bringing in pure Welsh stock.

No one lives at Bwlcheinion now, but there were aspects of the life there which, by our own materialistic standards, might be seen as sophisticated. One such was the daily delivery of my grandmother's newspaper, the *Daily Mail*, which was brought all the way up that exposed track and delivered at the door without fail.

It was a time when neighbours co-operated as a matter of course. The needs of sheep farmers made this co-operation both more prevalent and more necessary than for other types of farmer. Sheep need more regular attention and, where numbers were enormous, as they were on that difficult terrain, there were some tasks that could only be accomplished if all the local neighbours and their full contingents of staff did the rounds on a co-operative basis. One has only to imagine the labour needed to shear by hand those thousands of sheep which inhabited the extensive mountain land at the northern boundary of Ceredigion to understand why such collaboration was essential.

Wages were poor in those far off days and have not improved a lot since. Mr. Williams Wynne once received in his office a delegation of his farm workers, requesting an increase in wages. He looked round at them and said, 'Well, well. I can offer you all a good reference!'

Uncle Tom Jenkins had a servant, John

Thomas, who lived in at certain times. John Thomas was related to two shepherds who lived at Nant-y-Moch, in the one remaining cottage in the Rheidol Valley which was later to be flooded to provide the dam to serve a hydroelectric power generator, and which lies at the very foot of the Plynlimon mountain. To reach this cottage from Bwlcheinion, which lay south-east across the mountains, would necessitate a very stiff, twelve-mile walk. But John Thomas made the journey regularly.

His cousins were legends in their own lifetime and it was said, perhaps correctly, that one of them had sold his skull to the British Museum because it bore such a close resemblance to those of the ancient Britons. If any of these prehistoric genes had come down to John Thomas, I can only think that our distant forebears must have been amazing people.

My uncle Tom Jenkins attracted the attention of the late R. S. Thomas, the famous poet of the Welsh hills, who was then the vicar of the church at Eglwysfach. R. S. Thomas used to walk my uncle's land and described him in one of his poems as being 'carved out of the rugged hills.' Uncle Tom would never have seen himself that way; and his own sense of continuity was much more practical. He would often, while walking the trail to Bwlchymaen, point out a particular tree to me.

'Never cut that tree down, John,' he advised. 'It once saved one of my bullocks, when it tumbled over the side while I was moving the cattle.'

His farming enterprise was structured in a businesslike and profitable manner, but it was his cattle that interested me as a child, although they were not the important part of his enterprise. He kept upwards of a dozen females and usually sold their calves, when they were weaned, to good effect because his stock had a reputation for high yields of quality milk, and this characteristic would be carried by calves of both sexes. I have bought a number of young bulls from him for use in our Welsh Black dairy herd at Brysgaga.

His cattle were only used to seeing Tom, who lived alone. Tom usually wore a hessian sack over his shoulders in wet and cold weather, and when I called to buy steers from him, he always advised me to come similarly attired so that the animals were not too disturbed at my presence. The sack he wore was something of a family joke, and one cousin remarked, 'I hope he will leave the sack to me in his will.'

He kept some 1,000 sheep, for stocking was lighter then than it is today. He had very little in-bye land, and each winter he sent a number of ewe-lambs to Nebo, above Llanon, where the keep was better than his own but not so rich that the lambs would arrive back too fat to sustain an abrupt change of nutrition. Of these lambs, 100 were sold each year, either at home or at official sales.

Uncle Tom continued to improve the quality of his flock by the purchase of pedigree Welsh Mountain rams and reached a level where he was able to sell rams, too, under the auspices of the

Welsh Mountain Sheep Society, whose stringent on-farm inspections were carried out annually. He was the youngest son and had followed his father in the high standard of his stockmanship. If he sometimes played the joker, he could afford to.

Uncle hated any form of air pollution and if a vehicle arrived, spewing exhaust fumes, he would give the area a wide berth for ages. He was accustomed to the clean, pure air, and I am sure he would have been distressed by the amount of fumes given off by motor vehicles today.

Life on a mountain farm was not idyllic in winter. Often, my mother and I had to take Tom provisions from the local shop, driving in an early 4 X 4 Landrover. If the tracks were covered in ice and hard frozen snow, it was impossible to clear the sharp bend at the incline at the bottom of the Foel. We would unload everything and walk the rest of the distance, dragging large sacks full of loaves and other provisions. I remember visiting him thus, having struggled through atrocious weather, with blizzards obliterating the hills. We found him at home, sitting happily in front of a roaring fire, with his feet up on the fender. He had decided not to venture out and in answer to our question, had he been to see to the heifers up at Bwlchymaen, he replied, 'No. It's better that the heifers perish than their boss.'

His brother, John Jenkins, was sensible enough, too, for his herd prospered and he knew exactly which of their characteristics he valued most. He was a frequent visitor at Ynys and, of course, appraiser of stock. The best accolade he could bestow would be, '*Da iawn: y blewyn a phob peth.*' (Very good, coat and all.) The right quality of coat was vital to him as an indicator of general health and well-being; the rest of us would do well not to neglect its importance.

A bachelor himself, my uncle was drawn to the company of others like him. One of these was Charles Evans, Cwmcenrhiw. They shared a distaste for the growing trend of English families in search of a new life coming to Wales to buy local cottages and holdings. When these newcomers failed to make a success and withdrew whence they came, Charles would remark, '*Fe gawsom 'nhw'r ast*', implying the bitch had sent them packing. My uncle enjoyed this jibe, and capped it with a well known proverb: 'When poverty comes in through the front door, love goes out through the back.'

When it comes to uncles who were characters, I seem to have been richly endowed. I once telephoned one of them during a tremendous thunderstorm but failed to get a reply. He explained this later, when he said that he had been outside, showing the water where to go.

I have mentioned already, that from a vantage point at Bwlcheinion, I could sometimes distinguish a field or two near the Dyfi estuary which belonged to Ynys, the home of another uncle, Richard Evan Rees, who was the man who introduced me to pedigree work. In later years, when he was visited by a party of young farmers from America, Richard Evan Rees told them he had given his life to the Welsh Black breed, and I can confirm that this was no overstatement. His Ynys herd was founded in 1935, when he bought several heifers from D. W. Morris, who developed the Penywern herd.

My Uncle Richard Evan Rees once told me about a neighbour of his who was something of an expert in animal ailments. This man had been called in to inspect a lame calf. He took hold of the lame leg, to examine it, when one of the helpers told him that he had hold of the wrong leg. He replied, '*Efallai wir*,' (perhaps so), but still kept his hold on the first leg.

Ynys, which I loved to visit when I was a child, lies on the salt marshes of the Dyfi estuary, an environment that is vastly different from a place like Bwlcheinion, a mere few miles away, and each had its own challenges and its own tenacious incumbents. To reach Ynys, I would be put on the train, soon to be named the Cambrian Coast Express, at Bow Street and, many stops down the line, I would alight and report to the station master at Dyfi Junction. Later, when I was a pupil at Machynlleth Grammar School, rail travel was all a lot easier.

The station master would see me safely across the railway bridge over the Dyfi, ensuring that there was no danger of oncoming trains, and from there I would make my way to the farm. It is hard to believe today that Dyfi Junction was a very busy place in those days, as were the numerous smaller halts which served so many travellers, some of whom were just stopping to gather mushrooms on the marshes. All this was before the infamous

Beeching axe brought about the huge reduction in railway services and, significantly, before the increased use of the motor car.

The railway ran right through the farm and was part of its life and character. So was my uncle's friendship with the station master, a friendship which went far beyond entrusting his small nephew to his care. It was from him that he learnt the technique of transporting cattle by rail, knowledge which led to him advising other station masters on how to do this, on behalf of his friends. With Dyfi Junction right in the middle of his land, my uncle regularly walked the salt marshes to inspect his stock, and there was no better way to break his long journey than to stop at the station refreshment room for a glass of Guinness and a chat.

Making my way from the station to the farm was an education in itself. One needed to develop a sixth sense, to know exactly where the going was safe underfoot, and exactly where to turn, to cross the dikes and ditches. Certainly, it could confuse the visitor. My uncle used to do business with a farmer who lived not far away and visited Ynys on horseback. Each time this farmer approached the farm, my uncle would gesticulate from afar, giving him directions on a safe approach, i.e. where to come across the river at a shallow point.

'This is the only time,' he quipped, 'that I ever have any authority over you.'

Last time I walked the old familiar paths, after many years, I had to start along the railway from Glandyfi. As I approached Dyfi Junction, a wild curlew nose-dived, to drive me away from her young chick hiding in the marshes.

Ynys stands at the conjunction of three counties: Meirionydd, Ceredigion, and Trefaldwyn (Montgomeryshire). My uncle said he could hear the cocks crowing in each of them. In each of them, too, he cut sheep-grazed turf for lucrative sale, and, within a short time, it would green over again. My son Rowland, at Brysgaga, indulges in the same sideline today.

Six miles from the open sea, as the crow flies – but a lot further if one follows the meandering river as it creeps across the plain – Ynys was exposed to the influence of the powerful tide-race at Aberdyfi. If there was heavy rain and the wind was behind the incoming tide, the estuary would flood and the tide could come to within twenty yards of the farmhouse, depositing flotsam and rubbish every time. There was a rise of three feet in the tide-height after the improved sea defences at Ynyslas deflected the flow, and there was even an occasion when a 100-ton boat out of Aberdyfi was planted firmly on the railway line.

My uncle was never without a tide-table; he kept an eye on the rain and the wind, with reason. He was a county councillor and travelled often to meetings, by train, of course, but he was ever conscious of weather conditions and was constantly to be caught consulting his watch and his tide-table. Moving the stock, to meet exigencies of tide and storm, was something which had to be done in good time, and when trouble was brewing, he would leave messages with the staff to clear the marshes of sheep and leave the gates open, so that they could retreat to the high ground beyond the tidal bank.

It was a way of life and a living. Ynys supported 35 Welsh Black suckler cows, registered and milk-recorded. The sheep numbers were substantial, by the standards of those days especially, though my uncle raised no replacement stock and, to that extent, might be said to have maintained a flying flock.

The farm had assimilated a number of smaller homesteads, now in varying stages of disintegration. Only one still had a viable house, occupied by the farm bailiff, but they all bore signs of earlier habitation and this was enough to stimulate the imagination of any child. There was a pair of lime kilns, not far from the farmhouse. Both the lime and the coal for burning it were imported by sea; indeed, the Welsh coast is dotted with such old kilns. The tidal reach to the land of Ynys permitted the carriage by water of the raw materials needed for the kilns.

Each of these abandoned holdings had its own little orchard, and some were fascinating places. My aunt sent me to visit them, to pick fruit for the jam she used to make. My aunt used all the fruit and the wild mushrooms that grew on the bog. She also had a house-cow, and there was a patient horse, circling the shaft to turn the butter-churn. I could be useful to this process and was happy to taste the marvellous butter-milk at the end of it. The postman always enjoyed his glass, and looked forward to it every morning.

There were also rabbits to be had. I had been given instruction in the art of snaring by an old farmhand at home and was eager to prove my expertise. Without a word to anyone, thinking I would surprise them with proof of my skill, I set to work. Alas, it happened to be a Sunday and my aunt was incensed at this breach of the Sabbath. That ended my rabbit-snaring at Ynys.

My aunt played the organ at the chapel in Pennal, where my uncle was a deacon, and I would be greeted with, 'And here is the young deacon from Bow Street.' The Sabbath, indeed, was so scrupulously observed at that time, that no work was done at all, beyond milking and stock-feeding. The hay would be left out, whatever the weather; nothing else in the way of work would be done. One by one, the farmers lapsed, and it is now common practice to work regardless of the day, which means that every day is identical to all the others in the week, which is a pity in many ways. It has led to the decline of church and chapel congregations, to the detriment of the communities they helped to support. My father was a keen chapel-goer, except at lambing time. A critic of his occasional back-sliding once drew his riposte,

'Which is better, attending chapel or tending the flock?'

There is a tale of one preacher who arrived at chapel one Sunday morning, having been invited to preach, when he found, to his dismay, that only one person had turned up for the service, a rather religious farm worker. The minister waited a while and when nobody else arrived he asked the man whether it was worth carrying on with the service and sermon.

'Well,' said the farm worker, 'when I take hay to the cattle and if only one turns up for it, I do give it some.'

The preacher, succumbing to the inference made by the man, but rather irritated with him, decided to give him a double dose. He preached for over an hour, and at the end of the service he enquired of him whether he had enjoyed the sermon.

'When I feed the cows, Minister,' he replied, 'and if only one comes up for the feed, I don't unload the whole lot in front of just the one.'

On reflection, I see that my childhood covered the beginning of a loosening of the Sabbath discipline, which is sad but, perhaps, was inevitable. In those years the Welsh Black Cattle Society was growing in spite of the physical difficulties of attending shows and sales. Near to Ynys was a number of established breeders of very high repute: at Tyhen, Neuadd-yr-Ynys, Cerrig-y-Trane, and Penywern. Through my uncle, I became part of the younger generation of this circle of enthusiasts, indeed, it is with some pride that I contemplate an old photograph of all of us sharing a table at the society's 50th anniversary dinner.

CHAPTER TWO
Planting Ideas for the Future

It was in 1935 that my uncle Richard Evan Rees took the plunge into selective breeding of Welsh Black Cattle with the purchase of three pedigree heifers from David William Morris of Penywern, a farm and herd to be taken over by the Williams family soon afterwards. It was a foremost herd, even then, and eminently suited to start my uncle on his path as a cattle-breeder. The Morris family became famous, later, for producing a professor of agriculture (Dai) and an MP (Sir John), but my own special connection with them was the fact that Mrs. Morris had given me a start in life, too, of another kind but vital all the same: originally a midwife, she had delivered me into this world.

My uncle Richard's first pedigree calving was an event to remember and he told the story often. During her gestation, great care was taken of the mother-to-be, and as soon as the calving started, the heifer was assisted to deliver her calf. I should just mention that Welsh Blacks usually manage to give birth on their own, without help. The excitement was tremendous, not least that of Titus Jones, the enthusiastic herdsman. My uncle was

the manipulator and he pulled out a heifer calf but, on inspection, he noticed that there was another, a heifer calf, again. This was followed by yet another. That heifer had managed to produce three healthy heifer calves, and what more can you want? Titus Jones, believing in miracles, urged my uncle Richard, 'Have another look; there must be more.' Inexplicably, it was the plainest heifer of those triplets which brought the best progeny.

What creates the stuff of legend is the occasional bull which is not sold on but lives out his life on the farm; is successful; and, above all, has that elusive quality which makes for respect between man and beast. Garni, properly called EGRYN GARNEDD, was an early bull in the history of my uncle's herd, following on from VAYNOL DUKE, that was pronounced the best bull in the area but never shown because of wartime restrictions. Bought in from the famous Moses Griffiths, when he was nine months old, Garni was rated ugly. '*Creadur Hylla'r Deyrnas,*' (The ugliest creature in the Kingdom) is what my father said when he saw him and no one would

Author's uncle Richard Rees at Ynys, with 16 silver cups, a silver tray and a rose bowl, won at various shows in 1954, for Welsh Black Cattle & Welsh Black Prize bull, Egryn Garnedd

believe my uncle's prediction that ugly little Garni would one day make a champion.

He was shown successfully for seven years running and was champion four times. Garni began his show career by taking the overall championship at the 1951 RWAS at Builth Wells, when Mr. J. O. Pritchard did the judging. He was

turned out every winter, at the beginning of the year, which kept him lean and sturdy and his feet in good condition; and he was not shown until he was four years old, two facts that were the keys to his long list of show successes. It was no wonder that, when my uncle's health went into final decline, the mere sight of Garni being led past his window to the water trough was enough to give him courage to bear his illness. There were other bulls and other successes but nothing elicited the same sentimental attachment as Garni did.

There are stories, too, about my uncle Richard and Captain Bennett Evans, who is remembered, amongst other things, as a pioneer of hill land improvement. In 1953, at the RWAS in Cardiff, my uncle entered the group competition, was awarded four first prizes, yet came away with none at all. The reason was that the rules had been changed and now stipulated that the group of four must contain at least three females; the Ynys group consisted of four bulls.

Captain Bennett Evans, on another occasion, played a trick on my uncle. EGRYN GARNEDD, unbeaten since the Builth RWAS in 1951, was being led in rather casually by my uncle, who was evidently very confident of receiving top prize. Captain Bennett placed Uncle's bull in second place behind another Egryn bull, EGRYN ap HEBOG, belonging to Lady Shelley Rolls, who had the Hendre herd, in Monmouthshire. I immediately jumped into the ring and contrived to get Garni to stand properly and show off his true potential. The steward, Mr. Llew Phillips, was chuckling to himself and I finally understood the game being played. EGRYN GARNEDD was moved up to first place and there was loud applause from the audience. Captain Bennett Evans had simply wanted to take my Uncle Richard down a peg or two.

The two men were always friends in spite of their occasional differences of opinion. Bennett Jenkins had had problems loading cattle at the railroad at Menai Bridge and experienced trouble with the stationmaster. On the next occasion, when he had more cattle to load there, remembering his previous unhappy experience, he persuaded my uncle to accompany him but my uncle Richard sent Bennett Jenkins ahead and again the stationmaster played hell with him. Then, Uncle Richard came along and, knowing the rules and how to truck cattle, soon sorted out the stationmaster.

First, he demanded that sawdust be strewn on the floor of the truck. Then, Uncle Richard insisted that the cattle be untied and allowed to remain loose in the truck, there being sufficient of them to pack them reasonably tightly together. This had been found to be the best way for them to travel. The stationmaster had met his match in my uncle and Bennett Jenkins was a happier man.

The year 1957 was eventful for Uncle Richard, too. There was the occasion when the RWAS was held in the Blaendolau fields. It was a four-day show and for three days things went well. On the fourth day, however, the river Rheidol broke through its bank and the public were able to go boating in the avenues.

It was in 1956, when the Bath & West Show was held in Cardiff. Just as placid and experienced Garni was about to parade past the judges, the loudspeaker suddenly blasted forth and the old bull almost jumped out of his skin.

Eventually, Garni was beaten, at Rhyl, in 1956,

by the bull YSBYTY IFOR 3rd of Hafod yr Esgob, Bala. The judge at the time set Garni on one side and proceeded to judge the rest of the animals. Some of those outside the ring were critical of this and said that Garni should have been judged and placed somewhere in the line. However, that was not the end of his triumphs for he finished top at the last show of that season, in Welshpool, and honour was satisfied. At the time such was his fame that the *North Wales Press* published a lovely cartoon of Garni squaring up to his rival, Ysbyty Ifor 3rd, before the contest.

In his younger days Garni was kept in a *beudy bach* with a stable type door, the top half of which was kept open. There was barbed wire over the bottom half of the door. In Glanmorfa was a herd of breeding cows and when one of these was bulling, as a measure of his virility, Garni would jump over the door, miss the barbed wire, clear twelve dikes or ditches, and serve the cow.

The show season lasted all summer and there was a total of some 20 shows annually, some large, some smaller. Merioneth Show was a very important one and I recall the time when two lorry-loads were exhibiting at Tywyn. I had the temerity to suggest to my Uncle Richard that he could have managed with one lorry-load since the animals in the second vehicle wouldn't do much. For my pains I received a severe reprimand.

Shows were sometimes memorable not for the prizes won but for unexpected incidents that happened before, or after. We had come back from a show in the north somewhere, when the police alleged that we had been in collision with an oncoming car and we received a summons to attend Tywyn Magistrates' Court. The case was dismissed for lack of evidence when it transpired that the police had the wrong registration number for the lorry involved in the incident.

On one occasion a comical situation arose at a local show. The judge in one of the breed classes awarded a certain exhibitor a second prize in every class. Somehow or other, he also awarded him the breed championship. None of us could fathom how this was possible, and it was amusing to listen to the exhibitor's response when asked by the press how he got on. I hasten to add that the breed section in question was not the Welsh Black.

During my show career with the Welsh Blacks, I experienced many ups and downs but during a show season, if one frequents enough shows, it all averages out and one must learn to take the rough with the smooth. If you win, say nothing – if you lose, say less.

The time just before a show is always tense and Uncle Richard sometimes grew impatient, such as the time when a haulier was expected, to collect stock for the Menai Bridge sale to take place on the following day. When the time had run on and there was no sign of the haulier my uncle, who had no telephone in those days, sent someone off on a motorbike to Cerrig-y-Trane, to look for the lorry. On another occasion, on the morning of the Merioneth County Show at Harlech, we waited at Ynys for the lorry to call. Eventually, the driver arrived, very late and apologetic, and said he had overslept following rather a heavy drinking session on the previous evening. Luckily, the breathalyser was not yet in use. It was already time for us to have been at the show ground and Uncle Richard had to telephone the show secretary and explain that the lorry had 'broken down'. The show continued, judging first the classes in which we had no entries. The cattle were entering the ring as we arrived, the secretary having decided to wait no longer. Undaunted, my uncle led his heifer from the lorry and into the ring. In spite of the beast being covered in all sorts of muck, between them they managed to win a second prize.

Not all my many relations were cattle breeders. There was D. Myrddin Griffiths, the brother-in-law who taught me a great deal about sheep. He bred all sorts of breeds, both rare and mainstream, and because of his wide experience he was much in demand as a show judge. I did the driving: we went everywhere, up and down the country, and everywhere we went he would have a different situation to cope with, some more difficult and unpredictable in many ways than would be the case amongst exhibitors of cattle. Sheep are easier to move, so there are more of them at most shows.

At any but the bigger shows the sheep lines could be pretty chaotic; the animals were often shown just outside their pens and could be quite unruly; and the exhibitors were nothing if not independent-minded. There were sometimes little cliques of neighbours who had already decided who the winners were going to be, and then it took more than just an expert, but a man of sheer indomitable authority, to enforce the verdict he had decided on. D. Myrddin Griffiths tolerated nothing that smacked of fraudulent tactics or even carried a whiff of Spanish custom, and, despite the consternation this could cause, Myrddin insisted on examining exhibits from the right side of the halter, i.e. the side opposite the handler. This was the only way to go about it, and what a wonderful induction it was for me.

In my own show-judging days I would be confronted with the same kind of thing. On one occasion, I was challenged as to why I had placed a certain exhibit a long way down the line. I could almost sense D. Myrddin Griffiths standing behind me.

'That's where it belongs,' I told them. Dissatisfaction was palpable and I confess that I was not sorry when, at a later show, the same animal was placed even lower in the ranking.

Judging sheep was a very different business from judging cattle but serious all the same. Shows are part of the business of improving the overall level of all stock. I was to realise, later on, with WQL, that the national ewe-flock needed advancing by all possible means and showing is one way in which to bring this about.

Soon, my Uncle Dick at Ynys had Welsh Black cattle as exhibits for shows and as stock for pedigree sales. I must impress on my readers that a statement like that, made today, would merely mean that a suitable standard of breeding had been reached, and the question of transporting the stock to the required destination would, surely, be the easy part. It was not always so. In the first half of the last century it was an exercise in logistics, and without generous co-operation between breeders none of it would have been possible at all. I can only say that I hope this spirit of mutual help may soon return, for hard times can also produce a few good things.

The most frequent sale-venues at that time were Carmarthen, in the south, and Menai Bridge, in the north. The half-dozen or so breeders of Welsh Blacks in North Ceredigion, sharing a lorry and gathering stock from each farm, usually arrived at the venue in the evening, and the cattle had to be unloaded and bedded for the night. Then, council members held their meeting. It was one of the rare occasions in the farming year when old friends met to exchange news and gossip. It is tempting to marvel at their stamina but it was often the occasion itself that kept us going. I was one of the many attendant youngsters who never wilted.

During the 1939-45 war years access to Anglesey via the Menai suspension bridge was guarded by the army, and on the occasion of a Welsh Black Society sale at Menai bridge the Commander in charge was Captain David Rees of Brynbŵl, Borth. It had been a late spring, bad weather had delayed the seasonal planting, and everyone was anxious not to waste time. Mr. J. M. Jenkins explained to Captain Rees that he was well behind with his ploughing and Captain Rees said he would see what could be done. He managed to

arrange the release of one of the local men, who was able to help Mr. Jenkins finish ploughing in time for the spring sowing. It was always a pleasure to meet up with neighbours at times like these.

Those two venues that were popular in the early days have lost their importance now. Menai Bridge was invested with endless stories, some of which have taken on the aspect of legends. History has it that the first Menai Bridge fairs were held on the bridge itself; not the present bridge, but the much older, original one, built in 1827. Indeed, the third sale in the history of the Society was held there in April 1917. The story goes that, on one occasion, a storm blew up and the old bridge started creaking and swaying in the rising gale, with the breeders clinging on rigidly to the side of the bridge with one hand and hanging on desperately to their cattle with the other. These breeders refused, despite all entreaties, to move off their perilous perch.

The matter was the subject of endless discussion; some cynics said that the old boys were too scared to move, others maintained that that they stayed where they were so as not to endanger their cattle. I think I know which version came closest to the truth. We are deeply indebted for the example of fortitude set by these staunch men.

It was this same class of breeder who, some time later, when the breeding of pedigree animals held no premium over commercial sales, stuck to it and continued to breed their Welsh Blacks pure. They saw, in their wisdom, that crossing cattle is

The way it used to be. A street fair, probably at Cilgerran Carmarthenshire, before the arrival of the motor vehicle

like driving up a one-way street into a cul-de-sac: there's only one way out and that's back again.

It was a privilege to have been young at such a time, despite the fact that the life was far from easy. We lads were useful at sales but particularly at shows. The length of a show ranged from 2-days to 4-days, and we lived in what we called straw hotels, somewhere under canvas, near the stock; or the tops of the lorries, where we tried to keep warm and dry overnight under tarpaulin covers.

The coldest of all the show venues was Smithfield but there was also the Shropshire & West Midland, the first show of the season. It was while I was at this one that I well remember the river glinting silver in the hoarfrost at night, while I took a brisk walk, in a desperate attempt to get warm, and I returned to discover that the old tarpaulin that was to serve as my bed cover had frozen rigid and it was hard for me to get back under it.

One of my aunts had evidently been giving this matter some deep thought. This was the same aunt who had been so cross when I broke the Sabbath to catch rabbits, and it was obvious that she had forgiven me for she had a brain-wave. She gathered together some old blankets and stitched them up to make what I called a Welsh Black sleeping bag. It was not just warm, it also kept out the exasperating prickles of the straw.

The Royal Welsh Show had no permanent ground at that time and moved around between north, south, and mid-Wales; the sites were chosen more for size and flat contour than considerations of possible freak weather. It happened, invariably, or so it seemed to me, that the freak weather arrived with the show date and the expression 'washed out' acquired a special meaning. Later, when we got our excellent permanent show ground at Llanelwedd, our appreciation could be tempered by the extreme heat caused by its special topography, for the ground sits in a hollow surrounded by hills, which shield it from wind but also from any welcome breeze. Sticking it out through one class after another, the steward, Dafydd Miles, bailiff for Moses Griffiths, wailed, 'Oh for a quart with its arse in Clarach.'

As for lighting and cooking, our early facilities would have made a Health and Safety inspector's hair stand on end. I have to admit, in retrospect, that I am still uncertain whether the absence of such people then was a disgrace or, just possibly, a good thing. Lighting and cooking were done with gadgets operating on paraffin: pressure lamps and primus stoves, with mantles and pumps and all the associated paraphernalia. One might think that there was not much that could go wrong with such uncomplicated equipment, but go wrong it did, either refusing to light at all, or flaring up suddenly and perilously, amongst all that straw.

We reached a stage, once, where every lamp and primus had conked out, whether through a broken pump, useless mantle, or some unfathomable fault. It was young Bennett Jenkins who became the star on that occasion by cannibalising parts until he produced one serviceable primus stove, to heartfelt praise from my uncle, who was growing hungry. This was also that glorious occasion when Titus Jones, swearing that the pig had never been near the '*domen*' (muck-heap), provided piles of excellent home-cured bacon. It is rightly said,

'Milk the show cows for your tea, and heaven is all yours.'

★★★★

As my uncles featured strongly in this chapter, I shall close it with two stories. The first concerns Mr. J. M. Jenkins, veteran Welsh Black breeder, of

Neuadd yr Ynys. It was in 1947, and he was receiving the championship winner's cup from the then Princess Elizabeth, when he asked her,

'Have you brought your boyfriend with you?'

To which she replied, 'No, not this time.'

J.M. Jenkins achieved the Grand Slam on three separate occasions, and that involves entering the winning Champion Bull, Champion Female, and Best Group, in the same Royal Show. Very few have managed this in a lifetime.

My next story is about Uncle Richard Rees. It was 1954, and he attended an early meeting of the Royal Welsh Machynlleth Show Committee in order to organise sponsorship for that year. There were many representatives of local councils and organisations present and these people voiced their 'token' support. Uncle Richard wanted them to give hard cash, not make empty promises, and he gave them a parable about an old lady who was unable to pay a bill and promised her creditor that his reward would be waiting for him in heaven. Uncle Richard pointed out that this was no way to run a show and token support would not see the job done. The show was duly held and almost flooded out on the last day, when a cloudburst and deluge created a quagmire.

CHAPTER THREE
Men of Legend

Many of my readers will be familiar with the A487 road running northwards from Aberystwyth, and with the village of Bow Street, four miles on, extending from the Lovesgrove intersection to the road leading off to Borth, a distance of a mile and a half. Bow Street has no less than ten minor roads, running off to east and west, into housing estates, private and social, to cater for a population of some 1,500 souls. It has a spacious aspect and, with many trees and greenery reaching maturity, an inviting one as well. It is an example of the best in contemporary planning, using the lateral development principle to the full.

I say this because I am proud of my home village of Bow Street. I have served for many years on its parish council and on the rural district council and have worked and fought for every phase of its expansion and development. The two chapels, two pubs and the local butcher have been there for as long as I can remember. In times past, before the arrival of mains water and sewerage, the village consisted of a long stretch of mud-walled cottages, whitewashed and neat, with little

quartered windows. Some spring water was piped from Brysgaga, my home, to a part of the village, and there were village pumps at the side of the roadway, and a few springs, a reminder of which is to be found in the name of *Spring Cottage*,

Mains electricity, promised for the end of World War II, was a long time coming to Bow Street. Meanwhile, there was an enterprising trader who had a generator of sorts and supplied limited power to a few adjacent houses and who would re-charge the accumulators for our wireless sets.

Of great benefit to everyone was our railway station. We also had a smith and wheelwright, and a wonderful general store, Siop Moc, which sold everything, including our wartime rations, and was the venue where the old miners, retired now from their toils in South Wales, foregathered for their *seiat* (Fellowship Meeting). This shop is the only reminder of those times to have been preserved, and perhaps the ghosts of these old men still inhabit it undisturbed.

Our family were registered with Siop Moc during the war, so that is where we bought our

The last remaining mud-walled house in Bow Street was once home to Siop Moc, where we bought our war-time rations. The house is still in existence and is being refurbished.

food rations. My parents always said that both Moc and his wife, Ada, were straight and correct in their mathematics. A young lad, having bought provisions previously, returned soon after to say his mother said the bill was wrong. Moc had a fleeting look at it and said, '*Cer a fe 'nôl at dy fam eto* (Take it back to your Mam).' The lad returned to the shop to repeat that it was still wrong. Morgan Owen studied the bill further and returned it to the lad, saying, '*Gweud wrth dy fam am fynd 'nôl i'r ysgol eto.* (Tell your Mam to go back to school again.)'

I recall evacuees arriving from Liverpool at the start of World War II and one of them, alighting from the bus and surveying Bow Street, remarked,

'This place reminds me of a glorified pub that has no beer to sell.'

There was a time when many of the cottagers

kept a few cows, which they would walk along the village, twice a day, or they might milk them in the small fields they worked. There was, through the ages, an element of self-sufficiency but most village folk, the *gwerin*, worked as day-labourers. I spoke recently with one of our older inhabitants who recalled the days when a quart of beer, served in a jug, cost 2d, and he wistfully compared this with the present cost of a pint.

Today, Bow Street is largely a dormitory village with a wide social mix in its population. It no longer boasts a railway station, or the specialist craftsmen I have mentioned, but its amenities include a supermarket, a café/craft-shop, a fish and chip shop and a post office, where the postmaster is a mine of official information as well as the fount of essential local gossip. In addition, there is a small trading estate, a used-car sales compound, a builder's merchant-cum-DIY store, an agricultural merchant who can get hold of almost anything to suit his customers, and there is a local garage, where the owner is always ready to cope with emergencies and willing to do a kindness.

As well as convenience and a surviving spirit of friendliness in the village, the school is modern and well planned and the village hall has gone through a number of improvements to enable it to accommodate all sorts of functions. The crowning glory, however, is the Football Club, now based on its own leasehold property and with a stadium to be proud of. The ground and stadium were developed by means of hard graft from some of us

and with some very handsome local contributions running into several thousands of pounds.

I have mentioned the wide social mix. There is a mix of ages, too. We have an old folks' home and a complex of self-contained, old people's flats. These are clearly so attractive to their residents that record longevity is the rule here.

It seems remarkable to me, when I look back, that a few people meeting once a week could co-operate to push ahead and achieve all these developments and to do this so consistently as to make a unified entity. There was more to it, of course, than the weekly meetings. There was even physical effort expended to get things going, if some exceptional opportunity presented itself. There was a period of many years, starting before my time, when there were no lateral developments but there were the little lanes: Cock-and-Hen Street and Threadneedle Street.

The one which remains to this day is Cross Street, leading to and beyond the entrance to my home, Brysgaga. Its correct Welsh name is *Lôn-y-Groes,* so named because a cross was erected at the top of the lane to mark the spot where Agam, a Christian, was murdered by a heathen. The cross is no longer there but it still defines the lane. There has been much speculation about the origins of the name Brysgaga itself, but the academic consensus of opinion is that its name derives from the Welsh for Agam's Wood, where *Prysg* means 'Wood'. Today, at the entrance to the farm there are trees.

The original farmhouse at Brysgaga was built in 1181, and much has been added since but its splendid, enormous centre-piece is its kitchen. This has been there since the original building was erected and is now fully two feet below ground level. It presents a challenge to any woman, unless she understands and nurtures its genius, as my wife Dorothy has done over so many years of family life there. My father rented the farm from the Gogerddan estate and it was not until after his death that I had an opportunity to buy it. It is where he set up his Welsh Black dairy herd, right in the middle of a recession, and it is where my sister and I grew up.

My stories about my frequent visits to my uncles, and the fact that, instead of attending the local grammar school in Aberystwyth, I was a weekly boarder in digs and a pupil at Machynlleth High School, may suggest that our family ties were tenuous but this was never the case. We were blessed with a secure and loving environment such as is not given to all children. My grandmother at Bwlcheinion was what I would call a Noble Lady, perhaps a little reserved, but many found her gentle and kind, she made people welcome at her home and she was always generous; my own mother was strong when disaster struck but she was warm and gentle and anything but distant. Moreover, it is a measure of the secure family life I had at home, that I was able, aged eleven, to become a boarder in Machynlleth without suffering pangs of homesickness.

My parents sent me to Machynlleth rather than Aberystwyth because Machynlleth had a brand-new school with excellent facilities and had an outstanding headmaster in Mr. Haddon Roberts. Also, my father served with distinction in the first world war and had observed the plight of young recruits from Anglesey who had not a word of English between them. My father had also travelled extensively in the Antipodes and had benefited from his fluency in both languages. While Welsh was my parents' linguistic heritage they still felt that their children should be proficient in both languages, therefore, Machynlleth was their choice for me, while my sister was sent to Dr. Williams's School for Girls, near Dolgellau, where she also received an excellent education.

Machynlleth, in and out of school, is a more anglicised place than the Bow Street of my childhood, at least, it was a town where English and Welsh were used on an almost equal footing; this bilingualism undoubtedly rubbed off on me, even though I was already familiar with English, for we had an English maid at the farm. I have always firmly believed that an early dose of bilingualism is a help to any child, anywhere, and am flattered to see that this contention of mine has since been confirmed, following academic research into the matter. It affords an additional dimension to understanding languages generally, and this is something which extends to other thought-processes as well.

Whilst we were at school, without any outside aid, we became trilingual. What we added to the

1946-7. Machynlleth Grammar School 1st XI Soccer Team
Back Row, L-R: Vivian Evans, Frank Vaughan, Gordon Mills, Arwyn Pierce, Ieuan Owen, Wyn Evans, Eric Smith
Front Row, L-R: David Philips, Arthur Evans, John Rees (Capt.), Mervyn Davies, Edward Pugh Jones

daily curriculum was a private language of our own, devoid of any grammar, with convoluted linguistic roots and with a logic so original that it would have been a greater challenge to the famous Bletchley Hall of wartime fame than any code their Enigma machine managed to crack. We called this *iaith ni* (our language). It is well known that bilingual children are good assimilators of further languages but we were inventive with our private language and the ways in which we used it. For example, it was even extended to christening boys with nicknames which had belonged to earlier pupils, not because their successors were in any way related to them but because they bore

1947-8. Machynlleth Grammar School Football XI and reserves
Back Row, L-R: Jack Gravelle, Eric Smith, Fred Jones, John Parsons, Gordon Mills, Erwyd Edwards, Frank Vaughan, Mervyn Davies, Idris Evans, Glyn Stanton, Captain Davies
Front Row, L-R: David Philips, John P. Rees, Wyn Evans (Captain), Arthur Evans, Edward P. Jones

some slight resemblance to them.

While at Machynlleth Grammar School I enjoyed all sporting activities and nothing would give me more joy than to beat the First Team girls at tennis. Along with Arthur Evans, I was picked to play for the soccer First Team, in 1943, when Arthur and I were only in our second year at the school. Arthur Evans and Peter Rees, my cousin, were later to become full amateur soccer internationals, and both played for Wales.

During the season, we used to play soccer very dinner-time on the school field, with one of the goals near the main A487 road to Aberystwyth. Mr. Dick Micah was the local milkman, and he used to stop and watch us. He always enjoyed a joke, and one day, when Huw, Llanllwyda, let in several goals, Dick Micah remarked quite loudly,

'Duw, Huw bach, put the net up in front of the goal.'

I was introduced early to cricket by the four Thomas evacuees from Solihull, Warwickshire, and went on to become both school cricket and soccer captain. As a reward for beating Newtown and Welshpool in the Schools' cricket competition, our headmaster, Mr. Haddon

Roberts, took us to see the Australians play Glamorgan at St. Helens, Swansea. It was 1948, Glamorgan were the Counties Champions, and they fielded a very good team. The Australians had one of their best ever touring sides, that included Bradman, Hassett, Lindwall and Miller.

Emrys Davies, the Glamorgan opener, batted all day, for 28 runs, and was last man out but it was he who kept the side together. This was no mean achievement, for it can have been no fun to face the Lindwall/Miller fast-bowling attack. They

Summer 1948. Machynlleth Grammar School 1st Team Cricket XI
Back Row, L-R: David Philips, ? Shepherd, Frank Vaughan, Glyn Stanton, Mervyn Davies, Islwyn Jones, John Parsons, Jack Gravelle
Front Row, Fred Jones, Arthur Evans, John Rees, Erwyd Edwards, Eric Smith, Peter Rees

fared no better against the strong Australian side than most County sides and were all out for 198 runs. On the following Monday, Hassett scored heavily, dissecting the Glamorgan field, finding the gaps in spite of the field being constantly switched around. This was Wales and the inevitable rain fell on the following day, saving the side when the game was declared a draw.

St. Helens is no longer a major venue for home matches, since the development of Sophia Gardens, in Cardiff, which is now the H. Q. of Glamorgan Cricket Club. An annual match is still played at St. Helens, and in 2002 I was there for the first time since 1948. It is amazing how those 54 years have flown by.

The knowledge my father acquired during his travelling days brought him into closer contact with our landlord, Sir Lewes Pryse, owner of the Gogerddan estate, of which Brysgaga was a part. On behalf of Sir Lewes Pryse, my father was able to carry out inspections and conduct negotiations with outside bodies, e.g. the Electricity Board, from whom he extracted a promise of early connection for Bow Street in return for permission to run their lines over the land of the estate during the war, and eventually, the two men established a respectful relationship which was sincere and mutually beneficial. Nevertheless, my father gave no particular priority to the work he did for Gogerddan's squire; his life's work was the development of his farm.

In connection with Gogerddan, there is the story that a local man reported hearing from Mr Ceredig Davies, who was at one time huntsman at the Plas and also Sir Lewis and Lady Pryse's right hand man. At one time, a tramp was employed to help with outside work and, one day, a bull broke out of the bull shed and they were unable to catch him. The bull ran along the river bed as far as the bridge, whereupon it turned and retraced its steps. The tramp was experienced enough to hide behind a tree and as the bull came past, he ripped its belly open with his knife. Possibly he had trained with the Ghurkhas during the war. No one looked down on this individual from then on but granted him a lot of respect.

Ifor Davies, a local poet, related years later that, when out shooting over my father's land, he often came across my father and they would engage in conversation and my father would recount stories of his travel exploits around the world. He would suddenly break off, look up and make a remark on the condition of the grass, that the wind was doing it no good, or some other *non sequitur*.

The Gogerddan estate once encompassed a very considerable area of land. In past centuries it had extended from Pembrokeshire to the Dyfi and its land holding in Cardiganshire alone was in excess of 30,000 acres. At the time when my father settled at Brysgaga Gogerddan still possessed a great deal of fertile land north of Penglais hill, rising on either side of the valley of Nant Seilo and its tributaries to the forested foothills of Plynlimon. The Gogerddan mansion, a fine and substantial seat, stood at the foot of the valley. The tenanted farms were numerous and, standing on such geologically mixed terrain, they were very varied in character. To be prosperous such an estate needed energetic and dedicated management and sufficient capital resources. Gogerddan had neither.

Its occupants had not moved forward at all and seemed to think that they had a time-honoured entitlement to live only for their leisure pursuits, some of which were expensive. The Gogerddan Pryses were kind, in a paternalistic way, to individual tenants and did what they conceived to be their benevolent duty. A living had been maintained for some time at their expense, with its Anglican church and school, at Penrhyncoch. As an appendage to the Anglican church at Llangorwen, there was a little school for small children in the centre of the village, not far from Brysgaga, and known as Ysgoldy Lady Pryse, presumably named in honour of an earlier patroness. This was also the place, I remember, where my father went to pay his rent to Sir Lewes, to a chorus from the children, in deference to their landlord, of the rousing old song, *For he's a jolly good fellow*. The children sang this without the slightest inhibition since they were long accustomed to seeing the great man's portrait in pride of place on every mantelpiece, in every cottage and farm on the estate, and dusted hastily whenever he was expected to call at the door, or appear in the vicinity.

Gogerddan had a finger in every pie. There was the Gogerddan Hunt and the Gogerddan Hounds, whose breeding was farmed out to tenants, who, in due time, brought the puppies they had raised

to a show organised by the landlord and his lady, within the context of a fête for which they dispensed the wherewithal to pay for the entertainment as well as provide prizes for the best pups. It all created great enjoyment, including affectionately remembered incidents like the one where a foxhound recognised and greeted my mother, who had raised him.

'*Ble wyt ti, WOODSTOCK BACH?*' she said. He recognised her voice after two years and rushed out of the pack and towards her.

In return for help with the harvest at the local farms, known by us as *tatws duty*, each family had the privilege of growing a few rows of potatoes of their own, in various fields, in rotation. This was the time that saw the approach of the end of a long established era of the Welsh countryside and in the lives of those who managed and worked it, and even when I was a child, in the nineteen-thirties, the lives of the *gwerin* proceeded in sympathy with it. This was, perhaps, not exactly true of some who lived on the outer fringes of the estates, where were found former lead miners, who had often sought a living but not found a decent life in the mines of South Wales, and where chapel life offered stern resistance to the parish church and, more especially, to its school. One small community where the chapel held sway even founded its own Welsh school on non-conformist lines. At the inner core of the estate, however, there was the loyalty and affection I have described. It was an environment in which my father enjoyed a prominent position.

By the early nineteen-fifties, when Sir Lewes died, the estate had run out of money. A joint bid by the tenants to buy it failed because they had no purchaser for the mansion, and the estate was bought by the University of Wales, Aberystwyth, and became the Welsh Plant Breeding Station (now called IGER), soon to be world-famous, which provided increasing employment opportunities as it expanded. The tenants who had occupied the outer fringes of the estate bought their holdings cheaply enough because there had been no maintenance and the rents themselves had remained unaltered for as long as anyone could remember. The purchase of a prosperous farm like Brysgaga would be a different matter but that belongs to a later part of my story.

In 1948 my father was involved in a very serious accident, from which he only partially recovered, and life became a struggle for us until I grew older. I was just sitting my A-Level examinations at the time and was expecting to be called up to the Royal Air Force, to do my National Service. My mother and I hoped that my father would begin to recover and be able to manage the farm himself and I duly went to join the R. A. F. and begin training as a medical orderly. On the day when I trudged down to the station on my way to begin National Service, our neighbour, John Jones of Gaerwen, father of Vernon Jones, kindly accompanied me as far as the station and saw me aboard the train, a gesture that I appreciated very much. Sadly, my father's condition deteriorated and I had to seek release on compassionate grounds, so that I could come home again. It took a while before I learnt to shoulder the responsibility for what was now a sizeable family enterprise. My father was still there to help and advise me in the beginning but it was a chastening experience for me.

In 1954 he died. I continued milking the Welsh Black dairy herd, now gradually and due to outside pressures giving way to Friesians. My heart was always in Welsh Black pedigree breeding and I was able to circulate among the cattle friends I had grown up with through Garni and his triumphs and, through their generosity and my own persistence, I remained at the centre of events. I went on learning as the Welsh Black scene grew more sophisticated than it was when Uncle Dick Rees first entered it.

It was heartbreaking to have to take the dairy herd through a gradual transition from Welsh Blacks to Friesians. In those early hand-milking days there was another factor that was important: familiarity, one could almost say intimacy, with every cow, and knowledge one had of each of them. These Welsh Black cows were bred on the farm, registered and milk-recorded. We had used Welsh Black bulls, bought largely from my uncles, to ensure milkiness and health. They had become a model of what the breed could achieve in these respects, and, as for quality, Welsh Black milk has a wholesome homogeneity not found in any other. However, farming is, first and foremost, a business and to stay viable I had to trim my sails to the winds of change, for I needed to make a living.

The price regime in operation then (and now) offered scant reward for quality; volume was all.

After the accident, I am sure that my mother must have known what awaited my father. When the worst happened she was like a rock but she was never possessive. A few years after my father died I fell in love with Dorothy and we were married in 1959. My mother gave me nothing but encouragement. She bought herself a bungalow in Bow Street, where she lived, tending her garden, until her death at the age of 93. She was our friend and confidante until the end. Even in my childhood she had encouraged me to flex my small wings.

Having been a pupil at the village school, I knew all my contemporaries well and kept up with them even after I went to school in Machynlleth. Today, our activities might be described as hanging about. They included pranks aimed at an old drunk, and being threatened by his stick; poking fun at the one and only motor car, which made its way coughing and spluttering down Cross Street. I cannot recall that we did anything worse than that but we got as much fun out of these limited amusements as some of today's children get from less innocent ones.

There were other differences, too, from life in the district then and now. I will give just one incident, which happened on my way to catch the train to school. The weather was foul and, afraid that I might sit all day in wet clothes, my mother had wrapped me up for the journey in an old, long Macintosh of her own. Off I trudged, with a couple of other boys, then, up came a late-comer, on his bike, head down against the gale, and knocked me over from behind. As I lay there in the mud the poor boy believed he had knocked over an old lady. His consternation and solicitude were amazing. I wonder what the same boy would have done had this all happened today?

My mother taught me to be discreet, a necessary requirement in a village where the family at the Chapel House had twelve daughters and every one of them was married locally. I was not quite so closely involved in village life as the other boys, which meant that I had more opportunity to do things on my own; this was especially enriching and remains with me as a lasting influence on every aspect of what I have done and what I do.

Unlike children on many family farms, the freedom I was given to enjoy myself was remarkably liberal, not least when we had lots of wartime evacuees. There were four boys of my age at Brysgaga and another three at a house in Cross Street. They all came from Solihull and they all played cricket. We played and played and I loved it. This was, sadly, a short-lived pleasure; in the following year we had three different children at Brysgaga, all of them girls, and this happened when we were at an age when the females of the species were the lowest of the low, in our ignorant, arrogant male opinions.

I have not forgotten my friendship with the Rev. Wallace Thomas, who came from Montgomeryshire to become our minister at Bow Street's Garn Chapel. He was young and used a

Pupils at Machynlleth Grammar School, circa 1945, after a performance of Shakespeare's Twelfth Night. The author is front row, extreme right

modern, everyday approach in his sermons, which had a great appeal for me and which led me to see myself, in a religious sense, as truly one of his children, *un o blant Wallace*. There was another aspect to this man, too: his love of sport. He played golf on our land, with me searching for lost balls, and he went swimming at our local beach at Clarach. All this exuberance and broad-minded outlook on life was new to me and I confess that something else that impressed me tremendously was his sporting appearance, when he went out and about in his marvellously colourful college blazer. I spent much time in his company and have remained the richer for it. This was the ideal minister for me.

The approval I had for Rev. Wallace Thomas was not shared by the deacons at the chapel, the older ones especially. They disapproved of his sporting diversions, his breezy manner and appearance, and, in all likelihood, they disapproved of his down-to-earth sermons, too. They allowed a dispute about his stipend to simmer on and on, unresolved; and they condemned his choice of bride, a local girl, who, in fact, was very talented and, despite all dire prognostications, became an excellent minister's wife.

I was only dimly aware of all this discontent in the background, and one thing I regret is that I have no recollection of the attitude to the minister of the parishioners themselves. Whatever anyone else felt about this jovial character, Wallace was the man for me, and I still feel some pride and, perhaps, even involvement, in his decision eventually to retire to the same house in Cross Street where he had lodged at the beginning of his career, because, he said, it was unique (*unigryw*) and the place next to heaven.

To attain a place in Heaven, at the time, was only a vague aspiration for me; a more immediate one was the bliss of acceptance as a player for the Bow Street Football Club. How this happened I really don't know. At fifteen I was the youngest lad in the team and the only boy to be so favoured. Most of the players were ex-service men, and the game was played for its own sake, which is the true meaning of sport. Following World War I, one of the first captains was Dai Davies (Dai Post). Other notable characters who came later were W. L. Bowyer and Alawyn Magor. After World War II, the secretary was Wyn Ellis, and he ran the team. Some of our players were still serving soldiers and Wyn would have to resort to getting them compassionate leave

based on his telegrams allegedly reporting the terminal illness of Auntie Nellie, a poor, mythical soul, who survived an untold number of crises. Alas, one unfortunate soldier summoned in this way discovered that his commanding officer lived right next-door.

The club had been active since 1919, when most of the team consisted of miners working at the pit-heads in South Wales, who used to cycle all the way home to play in matches. They were a rough lot with a tendency sometimes to indulge in fights off the pitch, a pleasure for them which was kindly overlooked by the local bobbies.

After World War I, Bow Street Football Club had no facilities of any sort. They played, variously, on the field where the new primary school now stands, on Cae Gaerwen, the property of Mr. James, Caergywydd, who had helped them time and time again; and even on Cae Mari, at Rhydtir, where there was a huge tree inside the touch line, a tree which became their secret weapon, once they had learnt how to outwit the opposition by bouncing the ball off the trunk with perfect precision. Years later Afallen Deg was the local Land Army hostel, and, of course, the girls had become friendly with the local lads and came to cheer them on. They shrieked with amusement, too, when I split my shorts: I still feel a faint blush of embarrassment at the thought of it. This spurred me on; I even scored a goal on that day.

Our local support came from everywhere, not just the youngsters. We even played on Christmas Day and Boxing Day, always supported by capacity crowds. This enthusiastic support was not given in vain. To begin with we were nowhere in the local league: we were up against good clubs like the YMCA, Trefechan, and Pen Parcau, but after a few seasons we made prodigious progress, until we topped the league for several seasons. Practice and, I suppose, the investment of a huge amount of time were what saw us climb ever higher.

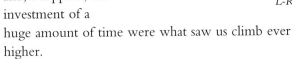

Science Laboratory, Machynlleth Grammar School, 1947.
L-R Hefin Jones, Eric Smith, Gordon Mills, John Rees, Islwyn Jones, Mr. Hugh

How I managed to fit so much into my schooldays I'll never know. My old headmaster, Mr. Haddon Roberts, was a man whom I still remember with respect and gratitude. Some schools, I know, give up on farmers' sons but Machynlleth School was not one of them. Somehow, I held my own throughout it all, even achieved some degree of academic and sporting distinction, and I learnt, not intentionally, but ultimately, a lesson that was worth a lot, and that was how to distinguish the 'wheat' from the 'chaff'.

It was not just my activities at home that Mr. Roberts put up with, but Welsh Black absences, as well. These were not all concentrated within the holidays and there would be an odd day here and another there when I had to forgo lessons, with occasional quiet collusion from my father. Not one to seek the wrath of anyone, let alone Mr. Haddon Roberts, I made full use of the eleventh Commandment, 'Thou shalt not be found out.' My esteemed Headmaster must have had a great understanding of another unwritten commandment, the one which I call the twelfth. It says, 'Thou shalt look the other way.'

CHAPTER FOUR
New Horizons

The great interest of my life was attending the shows. Given my liberal parents and my understanding headmaster, I was able to savour it all: everything the weather had to throw at us, our troubles with temperamental primus stoves and finding ways in which to satisfy our huge appetites. We certainly knew what to expect when we took our Welsh Blacks to show venues but we attended them gladly, with one purpose: the successful presentation of our animals to satisfy the judges.

The finished version of a Welsh Black that the judges recognised as a champion animal was not brought into being as a flash in the pan; its arrival at that stage of excellence after which we all strove mightily followed months and years of preparation. Successful mating to breed a champion is never a matter of chance. It does, of course, depend on the right mating but that is only a small part of the story. The consummate breeder has a depth of knowledge of his animals, founded on years of careful observation and assessment of related stock as well as all he has learnt from an untold number of mistakes. Like all acquired skills, it requires a special kind of intelligence and, above all, patience, to hone to perfection the skill of the top breeder.

These early breeders had developed all the skill and accumulated all the knowledge that went into the breeding of the best and the fine bulls they bred encouraged and assisted in the progress of the Welsh Black cattle. At a time when ordinary farmers rarely travelled around the country and were unable to make comparisons with their neighbours these few outstanding animals, seen at the show grounds, provided a standard to aim for. Not all breeders managed to come up with a top quality beast and it is worth reflecting on the tenacity it must have taken to invest in all the complicated business of showing.

The late nineteen-twenties and early nineteen-thirties brought the economic depression to agriculture, just as it did elsewhere. In many ways, though, the depression was more devastating in industries such as farming, where wages were already below the national average. To illustrate this point there was the case of an overheard conversation at the RWAS Aberystwyth, in 1933, where a breeder was heard to remark to his companion that the prize money from this show would be required in order to pay one farm-worker's wages for the year.

For the benefit of my younger readers, used to farms being run single-handedly, with occasional help from family members with employment off the farm, I ought to recall that no farm at that time could survive without staff. Some of them, certainly, were labourers, who went out into the mountain pasture with jute sacks round their shoulders. I remember that their bosses were not averse to wearing the same type of sack to keep off some of the rain. These men depended on the farmer for their wages and, very often, for their accommodation. As well as the labourers there were live-in maids to help in the home, with laundry and dairy work and anything else that could not be done by the farmer's wife alone. It is not easy to remember those days before labour-saving machines became commonplace, and to consider just how much labour they have saved, nor how cheap that manual labour was.

Let one story suffice to show that neither master nor servant had a life of luxury. The story concerns the servant of a comparatively well-to-do farmer, who was asked to select the plumpest, meatiest chicken from the flock, so that the fowl might be made ready for a feast in honour of the expected the return of the master's son. The servant spent a long time catching and assessing various chickens but it was noticeable that he repeatedly felt for meat on the wings. Challenged on this, he explained,

'That's always the portion left for me.'

It would be wrong to suggest that all farm servants were lowly or simple folk. Many grew in stature with the responsibilities they were given, or, often, simply assumed. This applied particularly to the status of stockmen, who were, by the nature of their work, considerably more able than many servants. Titus Jones, stockman to my uncle at Ynys, was one such and his involvement in the early beginnings of my Uncle Richard's herd have already been mentioned. Titus saw good females added to the three heifers bought in from Morris, Penywern, and then came the bulls.

My uncle had had the choice between NEUADD EMLYN and NEUADD CAWRYN, and there had always been that nagging feeling that, in choosing CAWRYN, he might have chosen the wrong one, and Titus had shared those doubts. Although NEUADD CAWRYN was runner-up to NEUADD EMLYN at RWAS 1947, he was the sire of YNYS CAWRYN, first in the Young Bull class that year.

Of all the great occasions, RWAS 1949 must surely have been the most memorable for Uncle Richard. It marked the first appearance in the ring of EGRYN GARNEDD, known always as Garni to the family, when the first prize in the senior bull class went to NEUADD IDWAL, third to YNYS CAWRYN, and fourth to EGRYN GARNEDD, bred by Moses Griffiths, but 'Garni' won the milk-recorded class; his dam, EGRYN HELYGEN XII, had given 1,200 gals in one lactation; and, to cap it all, the great man, Moses Griffiths, himself, confessed that my uncle had fed the wrong bull for the show-ring. EGRYN GARNEDD, Garni, Titus's great love and favourite, was shown at RWAS on seven occasions and was champion on four

After a relatively short time my uncle became a foremost Welsh Black breeder. He was such a wonderfully modest man that this unusual success had no effect on his personality. He was, in any case, already a man of some public esteem: a deacon of his chapel; a county councillor of standing; a J. P.; and a member of a whole stratum of established farming families. Indeed, he would soon become president of the Welsh Black Cattle Society, too. My uncle could take it all in his stride. Unlike my uncle in this respect, Titus Jones, the enthusiastic herdsman, grew with the Ynys herd until it became his entire identity.

My uncle died in 1961. I remember going to the farm soon after this and meeting Titus, who was cycling to work, his face awash with tears. His grief was such as we could never fully comprehend but his life and all that he cared for most had been buried with my Uncle Dick. The farm was sold and Titus continued working for the new owner. He was needed there, for his knowledge of the vicissitudes of the tides. Then, to the dismay of Titus, the herd was dispersed. Titus began to feel unwell, progressively so, until one morning, when he was on his way to work, he was unable to continue; he stopped to rest at a friend's cottage and died. Whatever it said on his death certificate, we knew that the real cause was a broken heart.

He died, fittingly, at the home of a very special friend, Dick, Penmaen Bach, a talented bass soloist and winner of the Blue Riband at Eisteddfodau on several occasions. Dick, Penmaen Bach, was, with Garni, something of an icon of the community at Pennal and the two were honoured together by a local poet. Each time Garni covered himself in glory, Dick, Penmaen Bach, would fire off a telegram of congratulation to my uncle, to mark the occasion. Two of the poems in their honour were printed in the local newspaper and put Pennal firmly on the map. I give them here.

PENCAMPWR PENNAL, MEIRIONYDD
Gyda llongyfarchiadau i Mr. R. H. Rees, enillydd Rhuban Glas yr Eisteddfod Genedleithol am yr eildro, ac i Mr. R. E. Rees, perchennog 'Egryn Garnedd', y tarw a farnwyd yn orau yn y Sioe Frenhinol. (A begio pardwn Ceiriog!)

> *Wrth ddychwel o'r Eisteddfod*
> *Fe gwrddodd tarw du,*
> *Oedd newydd groesi'r dolydd*
> *I weld y pencerdd hy.*

> *A'r tarw, gyda'r bryntaf,*
> *A ruai solo bas*
> *'Run fath â'r tarw cyntaf*
> *Enillodd ruban glas.*

Carlamodd 'Dic' i chwilio
Am loches yn y llwyn –
Hiraethai am gael dringo
O gyrraedd blaen ei drwyn!

Fe redodd nes dychwelyd
O dan y bedw bren:
I fyny'r aeth fel gwiwer
I'r gangen gref uwchben.

'O diolch, Egryn Garnedd,
Am ddod fel hyn i'm cwrdd.
A hoffet weld DAU ruban'?
Ond Egryn aeth i ffwrdd!
                                        D. L. Jones, Llwyngwril

RICHARD HENRY REES, PENNAL.

Fe daniodd ei nwyf, dinam – hen erwau
        Cerddoriaeth yn wenfflam;
        Deil yr odlau, aur adlam,
    I arllwys o fôr llais ei fam.

Gwynnach yw'r byd o'i ganu – ar binacl
        Rhubanau cerdd Cymru;
        I eurwych fab, ymdrech fu –
    Uchaf egwyl – gorchfygu.
                                        D. L. Jones, Llwyngwril

Before he moved to Brysgaga, my father had farmed at Gelli Taliesin, not far from Ynys. He used to say that the land around that area was particularly suited to stock-rearing and, if one thinks of all its herds of outstanding Welsh Blacks, he must have been right. Titus Jones, a worthy son of that soil, had his ashes scattered on the pastures which Garni had grazed. I am sure he would have wished for nothing else.

Jenny Buckton, who is currently compiling a book to commemorate the 1904 – 2004 Centenary of the Welsh Black Cattle Society, wrote to me, asking if I could identify the stockman holding the bull, on a certain photograph. The bull was EGRYN BUDDUGOL and the photo had been taken at Egryn Farm in 1930. Having shown the photo to some of my stalwart friends, I finally showed it to Mr Geraint Wynne, owner of the Ardudwy herd, whose father had been a stockman with Mr Moses Griffiths during the 1930s, when the bull EGRYN BUDDUGOL had enjoyed such a successful show career. He recognised what it was immediately.

Titus Jones was not the only stockman who grew into his job with elements of pride and authority. Another, Trefor Wynne of Ardudwy, was herdsman to Moses Griffiths at Egryn, where he started his job in the nineteen-thirties. When, during one of Moses's many absences, Lady Shelley Rolls arrived to enquire about the possible purchase of a suitable bull, Trefor asked her, without the slightest ceremony,

'Do you want a show bull or a stock bull?'
Equal to this, she replied, 'Both.'
'You can't have both,' persisted Trefor.

She finally purchased EGRYN ADDEWID, leaving behind the famous EGRYN BUDDUGOL, the bull that was Trefor's pride and joy over a show career spanning seven successful years. Trefor's memory and his legacy, too, are cherished by his son Geraint, who is now the owner of the well-known Ardudwy herd and affectionate custodian of Trefor's original breeches and leggings.

The inspiration for these remarkable stockmen were the men of stature whom they served, men like Trefor's boss, the legendary Moses Griffiths,

'What has the University of Wales ever done for Welsh Blacks?' he once demanded at, a crowded meeting.

'Produced Moses Griffiths,' came the reply. If that were all that could be said for the University's influence on the breed, it would still be quite a lot.

On one occasion, Moses Griffiths persuaded my uncle to let him have the use of Garni (EGRYN GARNEDD) to mate with Egryn Helygen 12th, who was actually Garni's dam. The poor beast had given over 1,000 gallons in one lactation and she was now old and dry, her quarters afflicted with mastitis. The offspring of this mating would certainly have needed to be given colostrum from another source than its mother, assuming that there had been a calf born at all. We never heard the outcome of this episode.

Every society needs someone such as Moses Griffiths in its make-up: a person who is that combination of brilliant, charismatic, and undoubtedly a little enigmatic. Moses was deservedly one of those people whose pride of place in the annals of the Welsh Black Society is taken for granted, not least by themselves. He produced a phenomenal number of outstanding animals, both for his own purposes and for sale to the owners of other herds, where they often became invaluable foundations for future excellent progeny.

Moses Griffiths confined himself to a very small number of cows, all of them proven and milk-recorded, and did not use a bull himself until he had hired him out to another breeder and inspected the resulting progeny. All of which, it is said, he financed with money made out of horses. It is unfair to the man to underestimate his achievement in any way. Behind all his success was as much perspiration as inspiration; and a very large helping of self-belief, sufficient, on occasion, to let him publicly revise his own stated views. An example of this *volte face* came with the controversy over polling of Welsh Blacks, which simmered on for years, with Griffiths firmly opposed. At the time there was an excellent herd in South Wales, the Island herd, belonging to the writer and naturalist R. M. Lockley, which had been polled by the careful infusion of Aberdeen Angus. One of the resulting cows, ISLAND BARONESS, was bought by Lady Twiston Davies of Wern Llaeth and subsequently offered at her own dispersal sale. Moses Griffiths it was who bought this cow.

Moses Griffiths did a lot of work as judge in the show ring, with unfailing aplomb. There was a famous occasion, at RWAS 1957, when he had a large class of females before him. Deciding between them was difficult enough, but in the middle of all this the VIP of the day arrived and poor Moses was put entirely off his stroke by the consequent disruption. He got the whole lot wrong, realised it as he did so but kept cool. He went off to greet the VIP, returned to the job in hand, and began calmly sorting out the class all over again.

Above all his influence was immense throughout the years he devoted to the Society's council. One may quibble at the detail of his policies and, perhaps, quibble at his frequent inflexibility but he was no maverick. Welsh Blacks have gone through some pretty hard times and the presence, if nothing else, of someone so positive, so colourful and so lively is something we all needed, not just once or twice but many times over.

J. M. Jenkins of Neuadd-yr-Ynys was seen by some as a counterweight to Moses Griffiths but that is something he never set out to be. He was the quintessentially practical man and he towered above us all in stature. There will never be another breeder of Welsh Blacks, of this I am certain, who can match his talent or outdo his lifetime of unbroken accomplishment. Born in 1876, he lived to the age of 102, and when he died in 1978 we all felt lost. He was truly the father of the Society.

He was present in 1904 at the amalgamation of North and South to form the society we know today and whose centenary we will celebrate in 2004. In the same year, too, he was influential in the establishment of the Royal Welsh Agricultural Society and its annual show. All this he had done by the time he reached the age of 28. Since then he served on just about every committee and subcommittee of WBCS, was President in 1943-4, and was later made Life President. Everything he did for the agricultural community was done in his inimitable, unassuming way.

He had a lot to be proud of. His herd, Neuadd, now run by his son, Hywel, and his grandson, William, has registrations in every WBCS herd book, beginning with Vol. 1, while his other son, Bennett Jenkins, breeds Welsh Blacks under the CARAN prefix, which is in turn run by the next generation, Bennett's son, Dilwyn, who is a very modern breeder, using the latest technology to good effect.

Jenkins, Neuadd, was a breeder's breeder. I would not hazard a guess at the number of herds which have been improved by the infusion of Neuadd blood. I do not know the secret of his consistency but, looking at the long line of his show successes, let alone his sales for record prices, it is staggering. I cannot possibly enumerate them all. For RWAS 1947 he bred the champion bull NEUADD EMLYN, and then went on to take the Grand Slam on three occasions. He took another one at the Royal Show of England

(RASE), winning every class, including the Group of Three with NEUADD IDWAL, EIRIAN and MAIR.

I met him frequently at shows, of course. Win or lose, he always had the same smile to greet you. What would surely have pleased him, though, was that NEUADD DAFYDD DDU 168th won RWAS three years in succession, from 1996 to 98. I fancied I could see the old man standing there when NEUADD ADDEWID 68th sold for the then record price of 8,000 guineas.

I have mentioned two outstanding breeders but there are many more. There are many, too, of lesser fame, yet they are serious breeders with a strong contribution to make. It has to be admitted that, in common with all other communities, we have had our mavericks, too. One such was Hywel Jones, of Glan Meddyg, a well-known figure at the South Wales sales. He had inherited a huge physique and was immensely strong. He farmed organically, which made him something of an innovator, and yet, he never de-horned his cattle, an aspect of the man that was backward-looking.

In the sale-ring, he led his animal from the front, with a rope round the horns, and the beast had no choice but to follow a lead that was backed up by so much physical force. Any display of recalcitrance was firmly dealt with by Hywel, who would grab the corner-post of the ring and tell the beast to pull as much as it liked. This called forth a roar of delight from the crowd. Hywel was always in good humour. Whatever the outcome in the sale-ring, he would always grin right in your face. If he had been lucky, he could be seen to be laughing all day. There was even an occasion when both the bulls he had entered at Dolgellau were rejected by the inspector. Undaunted, he put them into the commercial sale, achieved quite reasonable prices, and returned, grinning, of course, to the pedigree sale where he purchased the champion bull at the top price for the day. Tragically, Hywel died in a farm accident at harvest time. I attended the dispersal sale at Glan Meddyg, somehow conscious that his soul was there, looking down on the ring with that constant grin of his.

There were wags, too, who could be relied upon to proffer plenty of repartee in the sale-ring. Back in the old, rough days at Menai Bridge, there would be the Williams brothers of Tyddyn Ddu, Garn Dolbenmaen, heads tucked under their jute sacks, to keep out the rain. One of them, trudging the ring with little success, although they were good breeders, was asked by the auctioneer, Mr. McKenzie,

'What do you say, Williams?'

'Home, home,' he replied, to the amused approval of the crowd.

In the annals of the Welsh Black, two ladies played a noteworthy role in recording and registering animals, and I should like to mention them here. I quote from information given in a minute in the *Year 1973 Record, Vol. 62*, which records when Miss Pat Thomson was appointed by the Society to look after the registrations, taking over immediately from her sister, Mrs Higgins, 29 years ago.

As a nation we have many beautiful voices, a gift for the performing arts and a natural love of theatre, as well as a keen sense of the absurd. For example, I remember driving my Uncle Dick and he was urging me to moderate my speed on the road.

'Slow down, boy,' he warned, 'in case we meet someone else coming round a bend who drives exactly as you do.'

Welsh Black sales, the earlier ones in particular, provide an atmosphere like no other. I can remember occasions when the whole arena would be seized with uncontrollable laughter. I have mentioned the wags. This is another anecdote, which concerns a young blood, a foremost breeder, working in succession to his father, and he was endeavouring to sell a beast, to little avail.

'What say you, Vaughan?' he asked, turning to the possible purchaser.

'Iesu Grist, no. It's got a bum like Miss Royal-Welsh!'

Theatre apart, the sales were a rare opportunity for meeting fellow farmers, breeders and members of the family, to exchange gossip and news. The tea rooms, shabby, awash with slops and bits of sticky buns, had a magic all of their own. How far there was a conscious objective of a more serious kind: the observation of other breeders' stock, I would not like to say, but, to me, this is the

breeder's university. Here you see the good and the bad and the truly terrible, unlike the stock presented at the shows. The sale catalogue has been in your hands since it arrived by post at home, so there has been plenty of time to consult your herd books for breeding backgrounds. The auctioneers are hardly in a hurry: they go up in fivers, so each animal is in the ring for quite some time. It is vital, of course, to stand and stare at your own stock, at home, but unless you can develop the ability to make a good appraisal of a more general picture, you will not gain the benefit of appreciating what other farmers are producing.

The shows, on the other hand, are where you don't know the identity of the entries until you arrive. The calibre of the stock is more or less uniformly high. They provide a lesson in how to make the distinctions between the good and the outstanding. Unless you have found your way around the breed and are familiar with the characteristics that make for the best in breed, you will have no idea whether what you see before you is representative of the quality of a herd as a whole, or is a show team, put together for the purpose of pot-hunting, with awful stock at home.

Enlightenment is never far away. Those who are ready to stay by the ringside through the judging of several classes are well-educated. What is more, the judges know it, too. I have myself served in that capacity, from the smallest village show to the most illustrious, and have always been aware that the *cognoscenti* were sitting in judgment on me in the same way in which I adjudicated the entries before me. I should know for I spent enough time as a young learner, watching carefully from the other side of the fence, with those who are now old men like me.

It was when we were young, like the Society itself, that the unexpected could easily happen and often did. The breeders of Welsh Blacks were not the only ones who felt their way slowly to the levels of professionalism we see today. There was a bull, of a breed which shall be nameless, which was placed second in every class entered, but somehow ended up as breed champion. A judge, also nameless, gave a first prize to a neighbour who, it was said, tended his garden, second prize to one who mended his tractor, and third prize to a pretty young girl, in respect of unspecified favours, either granted or hoped for.

In an early, reprehensible practice show committees would entice certain winners to compete at their shows so that others would not win the challenge cups outright, which might be, say, after winning for three consecutive years. It even happened at one show that the judge enquired of a stockman, leading one particular bull, who was the owner of the beast.

There was, of course, inter-breed rivalry, even antipathy, and the Welsh Black men were not alone in their studied disdain for Ghost cattle, the name we gave to the newly arrived imported Continentals, a name first used for these imports by Sir Cenydd Treharne and despised in these

terms ever since. It happened to me once that, waiting to judge the next class of Welsh Blacks at a show, I was suddenly confronted with the arrival of a whole lot of these Ghosts. I am, I hope, of reasonably equable disposition, but on that occasion I was so incensed, that I ordered them off in unnecessarily peremptory terms.

The stewards, quite often, were lesser men who longed to be important and what little weight they had was duly thrown about, while the young folk waited for the opportunity to play some annoying prank. This even went so far, on one occasion, that the elegant bowler hat belonging to one very dapper little man was filled with cow-dung, straight from source. The gambit did not succeed as we hoped: the silk inside the hat was so smooth, that its owner simply shook it, wiped it, and left us looking stupid.

No show can be complete without the attendance of one or more VIPs. Most of them are nice, well-briefed people, who say all the appropriate things. The Spanish Queen was the VIP on one occasion, dressed in the height of fashion, at RASE, Stoneleigh. When invited to present the cup to the prize-winner, she enquired, anxiously, whether 'it' would be alive or dead.

There are so many memories I carry in my mind from those days when I was just one of a whole tribe of youngsters who were somehow connected to good herds of Welsh Blacks and all growing up together. There was more than fun, there was friendship. We were going forward together and benefited, undoubtedly, from all the expert discussions we had amongst ourselves and with our elders. When I look round at my old friends now, I see that none of us has taken received wisdom on board without modifying it according to our own individual, perception. By the time this early period ended, for the Society and for me too, I was well on the way to building my own priorities.

The beef produced by the Welsh Black has long been a source of pride. The idea that the Tudors, on assuming the throne of England, still had their Welsh Black beef sent up to London, is a measure of their good sense and something of which we are deservedly proud. The commercial, finished article is a good place at which to begin the subject and to give a timely reminder that, any breeder who ignores the beef, is going up a blind alley.

What conformation makes up the commercial beast was our constant subject of argument. With the growing popularity of leaner meat and the drift away from the high fat that was once the merit of beef cattle, the way we choose our beef animals has changed drastically over the years. Double muscling, so popular now, was frowned on in an earlier era but efforts to get rid of what we call sickle hocks were already under way. The market is what makes us do what we do but nature has a way of serving our ends, given half a chance, and my own inclination moved in favour of aiming for balance and the right kind of scale.

In Tudor times, animals and geese walked all the way to London, in front of their drovers, and this had bred hardiness. Wise men, years hence, were to liken them to stars of the sports arena but I had already seen, up at Bwlchymaen, that good feet and locomotion were not a fashionable new discovery. It has been said that a good bull should be able to get a good calf out of a gatepost. This is arrant nonsense. The good bull is nothing without a good cow and a milky one. Welsh Blacks have a longer lactation than other beef breeds and they are also a lot more generous with their milk. They are excellent mothers, right from the beginning because, in general, they calve easily, by themselves, out in the open.

Long before all this obvious good sense was preached by the great and the good it was second nature to me. It was not just because of Uncle Tom's cattle but also because my father made his living, like many others, from a Welsh Black milking herd. The milking herds served to encourage pedigree breeders to milk-record their cows, and the Society's super-register, based partly on milk, had been in existence for a very long time, so that the breed offered both good milking herds and good beef cattle.

Finally, there is the vexed question of polling. This controversy has persisted for ages and is not over yet. We do have a polled register in the herd book now, but it does not get the attention it deserves. The idea of ranching Welsh Blacks in Canada, Australia, and other places where there are tremendous open spaces had not yet gained ground when polling became a concept to me. I had seen plenty of the 'horned nuisance factor' at home in our milking parlour, or, 'those unnecessary appendages,' in the words of Capt. Bennett Evans, the famous breeder of polled cattle. It became one of my favourite hobby-horses and still is. I have to add, though, that in my case this was all it ever was. I found that I simply didn't have the scope, or the resources to embark on a polling scheme which would take years to bring in any return, if at all.

The adage, 'Input for high output,' does not describe the sort of strategy I entertained at the time but, couched in some other phraseology, it was coming straight at me.

CHAPTER FIVE
New Faces, New Challenges

Richard Evan Rees, my uncle who farmed at Ynys, was a member of the Welsh Black Cattle Society's Council, and its President in 1954-55, when I was in my twenties and eager to learn more about the Blacks. He was certainly a conventional man, and the insight I got into the Society's affairs was bound to impress me. I had nothing to lose at this stage by absorbing knowledge for, however closely involved I wanted to become, I was still not putting my hand into my pocket to translate any new ideas into reality. It has to be admitted, too, that I was often influenced in my ideas in accordance with my admiration for the men who gave them voice.

I admired and was impressed by Gwilym Edwards, our first full-time Society Secretary, who was greatly respected for his tireless application to his job, for forward thinking and almost single-handed initiatives. Gwilym Edwards held the post of the Welsh Black Society's secretary from 1951 until his death in 1974. A telling epitaph was contributed by Lt. Col. Price of Bala, who said of Gwilym Edwards that he was:

'The right man in the right place at the right time.'

His tenure spanned an auspicious era in the history of the Society; it is not too much to say that, in many ways, he was the architect of its future. He was appointed at a time when the Society's administration was in utter chaos. It had been handled on a voluntary basis by G. O. Thomas, a partner in our firm of auctioneers, and had then been taken over by Moses Griffiths who wrestled with the work to the best of his ability, from an office in a quaint old building in Eastgate in Aberystwyth. To reach this lair one had to climb a creaking little stairway, smothered in dust, often to discover that the office was empty.

The presence of the Secretary was necessary for very many day-to-day matters, such as the registration of a calf, while important matters like show- and sale-entries, with a definite time-limit, were rendered almost impossible if there was nobody available to attend to them. Apart from difficulties of dealing with the routine stuff, the Society's internal administration suffered from lack

Machynlleth, May 1955
Welsh Black Cattle Society 50th Anniversary Dinner of 1954-55, attended mostly by the then young members of the Society.
Front Row, L-R: Mr. Alfred Edwards, John Rees, R. H. Buckley
Top Row, ?, Mr. Williams, Morfa Mawr, Glyndwr Philips, Morfa Mawr, ?
Right front to top, Bennet Jenkins, G. T. Owen, Hywel Jenkins, William Jones, ?

of regular organisation. This state of affairs could not continue. Nevertheless, one wonders whether a full-time secretary would have been appointed at all if it had been known at the time that the accounts were in deficit.

On his appointment, in the Spring of 1951, Gwilym Edwards moved the Society's office to Caernarfon, where he was based and which was central to the majority of Welsh Black herds. At the AGM, in the autumn, he showed his true worth, for he had cleared all the administrative backlog and was able to present a set of accounts which showed, for the first time, an item of income, under the heading SALES, which represented the commission due to the Society from their auctioneers. At the same AGM he also offered proposals for amendments to the Society's rules as well as introducing one which was to lead to the creation of an established panel of judges. He had managed all this in something like six months.

By the next AGM, in the Autumn of 1952, Gwilym Edwards was able to put forward some new ideas of the direction to be taken in the Society's policy, its provision for the future and its ability to cope with, or even pre-empt, the changes which we all knew were coming. We were concerned at the slow demise of the Welsh Black dairy herds and the gradual move by many producers to Friesians to take the place of Welsh Black cows. Gwilym echoed our own thoughts on the matter when he said that their attributes should not be overlooked in the process of such changes and that every effort should be made to enable some breeders to keep their Welsh Black cows as sucklers.

He offered two proposals. The first aimed to tidy up the existing system of milk-recording, with its Register of Merit, now carefully graded and extended to male progeny. The second was an improvement to the Foundation Dam system, to encourage the pure-breeding and upgrading of females. Both these, but the second in particular, were vital if we were to move to suckler herds producing progeny of both genders which would be eligible for registration and to be traded at our pedigree marts.

What really set the tone for the coming era was, perhaps, the boldest move our secretary made

and this also came before us at the AGM of 1952. This was his Policy Proposal. Policy had never been formulated in a way which enabled the Society to look forward to a future outside the scope of the average breeder's perspective. This Policy Document lays down basic criteria of a hardy, milky and thrifty, dual-purpose animal and demands uncompromising adherence to them. It goes on to say, for Stage 3 of a proposed programme:

'When there are sufficient numbers available, to go all out, by every means available, to increase the number of new herds, not only in Wales but also in England and elsewhere.'

And, further, that (then)

'... the popularity of the breed will increase by leaps and bounds, resulting in an increase in demand and consequent increase in prices.'

I was not present at that AGM, but if this Policy Statement had set the meeting on fire, I would have heard about it; in fact, I have only just unearthed a copy of it while I was thumbing through an old herd book. It has been truly said that a prophet gets least honour in his own village. Gwilym was certainly prophetic but I suspect that, in this case, it was more likely that a grand design for the future would have had limited impact on a community sustained for so long by the trusted bedrock of tradition, certainly in those early days. Whether his message was well received, what he wanted to see happen did eventually happen, but not overnight.

The Society had some 350 members at the

time, of whom two thirds farmed in North Wales, and there were 16 outside Wales. This was when, if you made £65 from the sale of a pedigree cow, you were doing very well; it would take a champion bull to make twice that.

By 1974, which saw the end of Gwilym Edwards's tenure, there were 1,350 members, of whom over 200 were outside Wales. The average price per female was 250 guineas and the number sold had increased by leaps and bounds.

In the shorter term, it was Edwards's recognition that steps must be taken in response to the demise of the Welsh Black milking herd which had strong practical implications. Not many upland farmers were well-heeled men. The gradual replacement of Welsh Blacks by Friesians in lowland milking herds has already been mentioned; knowledge of this would hardly serve as encouragement to those still into Welsh Blacks to stick with them. The time was approaching when the suckler cow, albeit still prized for her milkiness, would cease to produce bulls which would be used to enhance the performance of dairy herds, still less would this apply to female progeny for a similar purpose. This lowland trend could have been the end of Welsh Black breeding on the hills and, with it, all the rest as well. It was Edwards's patient work which averted this with the help, it should be added, of a changing economic environment.

Something too easily forgotten is the fact that, for some years after the end of the war the UK economy remained on a quasi-wartime footing.

Austerity persisted; we were paying for our wartime lend-lease arrangements with our American allies and had declined to participate as recipients in the Marshall Plan, which had been on offer to the whole of Western Europe. There was still rationing of food and even of agricultural feeding stuffs. Even the old 'WAR AG.' lingered on, consisting of committees of local worthies who oversaw the use of agricultural land, whether suitable or not, for the maximum production of home-grown food. Farms could still be expropriated for what was judged poor husbandry.

With the arrival of the nineteen-fifties and the lifting of many war-time restrictions all this external system of controls and management slowly fell away and we saw the introduction of a policy of active support for agriculture. Its objective was to achieve a saving on foreign exchange. To cut down on imported food the government offered guaranteed prices for an ever-increasing range of products, free agricultural advisory services and easy credit for the purchase of a growing range of agricultural machinery. There was a rise in prosperity at a more general level, as well. People were able to travel more easily, wage levels improved, there was more money about and more optimism. The future for the Welsh Blacks seemed more realistic in the light of a rise in confidence.

What Edwards's far-sighted policy achieved was that, instead of gradually following a trend, breeders of Welsh Blacks became active and were able swiftly to capitalise on changes at their inception. The task which Edwards had set himself

Talybont Young Farmers' Club 1955

Back Row, L-R: Hywel Williams, David Thomas, John Thomas, Ieuan Evans, Hywel James, Vernon Davies, Vernon Jones, Ken Evans, David Jones, Trefor Jones, William Jenkins, Gwyn Jones, Geraint Jones, ?

Middle Row, David James, Wyn Davies, Gwyn Royle, David Jones, Harry Jones, Johnny Owen, D. J. Thomas, Johnny Jones, Humphrey Roberts, Handel Morgan, Tom Davies, Wyn Thomas, Henry Davies

Front Row, David Wyn Edwards, Ieuan Evans, Gwilym Jenkins, Marian Hughes, Margaret Jenkins, Elizabeth Royle, John Rees, Gwyneth Owen, Rosalind Edwards, Mair James, Judith Williams, Ieuan Evans, David James, John Hughes

was to persuade people to produce suckler cows and beef and stores, as such. His first prerogative was to establish contact with the Society's members. He visited as many of these as he possibly could for he knew that the right kind of encouragement was crucial. He approached each member in the same way, whatever his status, and talked things through in detail with them. This was the surest means to confidence-building and vital if the Society was to reach out beyond its core of established breeders. For there was a number of challenges to be grappled with. There were, in this post-war period, many commercial enterprises with no connection with the Society beyond the purchase of Welsh Black bulls; others were milk-recorded but this was patchy and increasingly pointless. Now that the suckler cow was the element on which the breed depended our Foundation Dam system, with facilities for upgrading, was of vital importance to the expansion of full-pedigree herds. This was the concept that had to be sold to members and Gwilym Edwards ensured that it was.

For my part, I met him often, through my uncle and at shows. And, even after my uncle's death, when I had no obvious links to Welsh Blacks, he remained aware of my personal aspirations and gave me nothing but support. His work for the Society can be measured in context if I quote figures taken at the beginning and compare them with those at the end of his time as secretary. In 1950, full registration was 788 for females and 188 for bulls; but in 1973, it was 5,732 for females and 388 for bulls.

The relatively small advance in the number of bull registrations has several causes. One is, of course, the demise of the Welsh Black dairy herd. Another is the arrival of artificial insemination, which is used especially in smaller herds which might not be able to justify a stock bull and certainly not one of the quality of the A. I. bulls offered by the Milk Marketing Board. This use of A. I. had not yet reached a stage where it might endanger the size of the genetic base; on the contrary, it offered a degree of variety within herds

Gwilym Jenkins, J. P. Rees, Wyn Davies, Marian Jenkins (neé Hughes), Elizabeth Royle Evans

which, but for the convenience of AI, might never have achieved a conversion from dairy to pedigree suckler at all.

Another cause of the low number of registered bulls was also to do with finance. Although pre-sale weighing and inspection was something to come in the future, it was still expensive to raise a bull-calf for presentation later as a prospective sire, so only the very promising animals were registered.

There was always the temptation to use other beef-breeds, to produce crossbred stock. This would, of course, affect the female stock as well. The only ways to avoid that were to try to attract more members, to raise the popularity of pedigree sales, and improve prices with it.

Within the Welsh Black heartland the growth in herd numbers indicated that the time would soon come when it would be imperative to go further afield. For this to happen the popularity of the sales was crucial, with a choice of good entries to come forward. Yet, throughout this time, and even in the nineteen-sixties, when prices advanced steadily, as predicted, the proportion of members offering stock at Society sales remained stubbornly at about a quarter of the total membership and it was to a chorus of unremitting dissatisfaction.

I well remember these gripes but wondered, even then, whether they were entirely justified. Membership-building, which was proceeding apace, also necessitates the slow process of herd-building, too, especially in a breed dependent on the brood cow, where there should not be, and was not, a predominance of 'flying herds.' It follows that, for the time being, the sale of breeding stock was still concentrated in the hands of the old-established breeders, who had long reached a stage where production-disposals were a feature of their business management.

As with everything else, popularity comes from keeping your name in the forefront of people's minds. The best advertisements were the shows. I have described the early ones and the sheer hardship we all had to put up with just to be there, let alone show our stock. Soon, all this began to change quite quickly. Shows, large and small, went from one record attendance to the next, year on year.

The farming public enjoyed easier access and so did the stockmen. There was more money about and greater mobility, too. Even so, nothing will ever change the fact that showing is expensive and requires a deal of preparation. More people joined the show circuit but, in the end, it was still down to a nucleus of top breeders with experience, dedication and, above all, stock to sell, to keep their herds in the forefront of the public mind. In the last analysis, what makes the shows possible is the fact that showing is a labour of love. Once one has become addicted to the habit, it persists for a lifetime. I say this as one who knows. In part this period coincided with the 'Garni' glory-days that I have described elsewhere.

In Wales Welsh Blacks enjoyed the same kind of popularity as local sports teams. At the Royal Welsh Show the main ring for the champion's parade would be packed for hours before the event, with people wanting to see their own side in pride of place, if possible as inter-breed winners. This happened more often than one might suppose. Later, a new English member was to remark, more truly than perhaps he realised, that the breed had advanced, like a football team, from the fourth to the first division. So much for the rescue-operation following the demise of the Welsh Black dairy herds. It was succeeded, again at Edwards's initiative, by a forward thrust which has, it is fair to say, set the direction for the breed for the future.

Welsh Blacks had been represented at the Royal Show of England for many years but the excitement engendered by a large entry and the backup of a society with good experience at advertising are basic requirements if a breed is to be noticed. Now, increasingly, both were forthcoming. Welsh Blacks were shown at more and more shows outside Wales, including less spectacular but specialised and prestigious ones like the Bath and West. We broke into the English market first, then we entered the really exciting one, the home of suckler cows, the Scottish market. We arrived at the Royal Highland Show. To help us make inroads over the border, Council was persuaded to purchase for us a caravanette, from which we were able to mount our promotions.

To attract big Scottish breeders took a degree of professionalism which might, in earlier days, have been outside the scope of our society. Now it was done. A handful of Scottish breeders joined in 1963 and, ten years later, there were over seventy. This was more important than such numbers might suggest. These were Scottish breeders of substance, who had sufficient land to maintain large numbers of suckler cows and sufficient room for selection to enable them to run concentrated pedigree systems with future projections of their

own. They went on to make an enormous contribution, and still do.

The Earl of Cawdor established a Welsh Black herd near Nairn, a stone's throw from the Arctic Circle, under the management of Mr. Morrison MRCVS, who became so enthusiastic about the ability of Welsh Blacks to thrive in the harshest conditions that he wrote a well known book entitled *Red Dragon Farm*, and lectured (in Wales) on his chosen field. Further south, in Berwickshire, Mr. Dobie started a large enterprise, using two prefixes for the naming of his animals: SHANNO and SHANOBANK, the latter polled, to develop a herd which would eventually be polled throughout and of top quality.

The Scottish stock-breeding fraternity has an in-built cohesiveness which has always worked to its benefit. By the end of Edwards's tenure, a Scottish Committee was already envisaged but long before that, from 1964 onwards, there was an annual outing from Wales to Scotland, where Welsh breeders, myself included, were entertained with characteristic heartiness and also introduced to the excellence of Scottish stock. It was fun but there was a wisdom behind it, on both sides. It bridged any differences of approach and tradition and ensured that there would be mutual respect rather than bitter rivalry.

If the Welsh invasion of Scotland was a master-stroke, more such were to follow. Exports at that time were going to the Antipodes and to Canada and the US. To begin with, and certainly during Edwards's time, these had provided little more than publicity value. Exporting live animals is expensive and the numbers involved could never be very large. Nevertheless, it meant that new herds would be started, under a variety of conditions, which would do more than expand the influence of the breed. It would eventually make a valuable addition to our local genetic base because Welsh Blacks are dual-purpose and can be kept in closed herds and pure-bred, unlike the Angus bulls, which were exported in large numbers to the Argentine and crossed with other breeds to make the 'Angus steak'. Surprisingly, this venture had the support of Council.

What Edwards could not foresee was the enormous benefit we would later reap from the arrival of new technology, which would enable us to offer semen and embryos for export, together with an objective data backup. It was, however, the foundations he laid at an earlier stage which enabled us to build on existing markets. His far-sighted vision of the future was as far as anyone else could see at that time. Throughout all this his day-to-day work on the home ground was organised to perfection, contact with members was never neglected, and the business administration was flawless.

Our breed journal saw its first publication shortly after his death. The office in Caernarfon employed eight people and ran like clockwork. The basic figures speak for themselves: in 1973 the gross total taken at Society sales had risen to £375,000. To me, Gwilym Edwards was more than the right man at the right time: he laid the foundations for other times to come. His strength lay in his ability to identify incipient trends and formulate new policies and in his willingness, even at the cost of making enemies, to act on them and do so decisively.

CHAPTER SIX
Reflections on the Glory Days

If, during the Edwards Era, the Society was helped to success by favourable changes in the commercial environment and reached a spectacular zenith in 1973; by the end of the following year, the year of his illness and death, there was a nation-wide collapse of livestock prices and, after a short-lived, artificial upturn following a Canadian buying-spree, those who had herds of Welsh Blacks suffered the shock-waves like the rest of the agricultural community.

Shortly after Gwilym Edwards's death it began to seem likely that I would be able to fulfil my dream of moving from milking to breeding pedigree Welsh Blacks. I have to say, in retrospect, that these economic shock-waves left me unimpressed. I can only think that Edwards had instilled in all of us so much confidence in the capacity of our breed to continue to go from strength to strength that this and the impending threat from imported Continentals received less attention than it deserved. For the Society to keep up a good rate of activity in the face of such exposure to a temporary downturn presented a very different challenge.

Dai Davies, the Secretary who followed Gwilym Edwards, was a very different man from his predecessor. Dai worked extremely hard to hold everything together throughout the 21 years of his tenure. The crisis of the mid-seventies was not the only one to occur during his term of office. These setbacks were due entirely to external forces and it could be argued that Welsh Blacks fared less badly than other breeds; but the shrinking figures for membership, registrations and sale entries were such salient and simple markers that your average Mr. Breeder could be forgiven if he saw them as the only criteria by which to judge.

Dai Davies put himself out, perhaps unduly, to indicate silver linings behind the clouds, as if there had been a slight, unspoken inference that he bore some kind of responsibility for these adverse trends. In fact, he attempted to explain them, though he wisely desisted from airing his private fears that the influx of Continentals and the establishment of so many crossing herds might well reduce the breed down to a supplier of suckler cows for such a purpose, with a price structure which reflected it.

It was not easy to pinpoint the progress which was made and which put the breed in a strong position once better times arrived. This was based on a forward movement in the quality of the stock and in the opportunities which presented themselves for innovation. Here again, Dai Davies ensured that Brinley Davies, of the Welsh MLC, and advocate of technological innovation, was a regular contributor to the journal. Dai and Brinley had their eyes on the future and tried to bring us all to see the same vision of it that they saw.

Dai Davies was, above all, a servant of the Council and, unlike his predecessor, did not exceed his brief. It was not until he wrote his valedictory remarks, on his retirement in 1994, that he allowed us a glimpse, no more than that, of the personal concerns he had felt. His epitaph encapsulates his many attributes.

Dai Davies

Yma Gorwedd Dafydd
Adroddwr Stori Celfydd
Diddanwr a Chanwr o Fri
Mae Hiraeth ar dy ôl Di

During Mr Dai Davies's time as secretary he confided in me by saying that, for 21 years, the two bulls that had the biggest impact were PENYWERN SERAFF 18th and IWRCH SERAFF 2nd, his grandson. I believe him.

Another bull to make its mark was PENNAL MEIRION 6th, who was widely used through AI. Initially, PENYWERN SERAFF 18th, bred by Williams, Penywern, was purchased by Mr T W Williams, Caerynwch, in a Dolgellau sale, for the then record price of 3,500 guineas, when he was only 3rd in class. Mr T W Williams kept him for four years and although he was a proven bull, having sired many stock bulls, he tried twice, unsuccessfully, to sell him at the Dolgellau Sale.

Eventually, he was sold to Mrs Weiner, a Jewish lady who farmed near Bedford, in the Home Counties; a few years earlier she had won the Burke Trophy for the best pair beef at the RASE, with a pair of Longhorns. She was keen, she had a tiptop cowman, and she was intending to win everything with her Welsh Blacks but it was not to be because her cowman lost his health and she decided to sell up all her stock. At that time I asked Mr Davies, the Secretary, if he knew of a good bull for sale and he mentioned Mrs Weiner and PENYWERN SERAFF 18th. During his lifetime the bull had been a prolific stock getter, throwing many good young bulls. I immediately contacted Mrs Weiner, who wanted me to see her bull. I replied that I had already seen enough of him. He was now 6 years old and she was asking 2000 guineas for him, which was rather much for what was quite an old bull. Eventually, she decided to sell all her Welsh Blacks, at a multi breed sale in Chippenham, conducted by John Thornborrow. I was unable to go to the sale because I had a meeting in Birmingham, and I sent

Penywern Seraff 18th

my son, Rowland, accompanied by a friend, to buy the bull.

The Welsh Blacks at the sale made more money than the other breeds, with PENYWERN SERAFF 18th topping the sale at 1500 guineas. Colonel Bomfrey of Cowbridge, who had Marchiangos, brought the bull back to South Wales and I fetched him home next day. Colonel Bomfrey had massive bulls, housed in big sheds, but he had never seen such a massive Welsh Black as Seraff 18th, who weighed 27 hundredweight at the time. Seraff 18th threw good stock and I sold many stock bulls out of him. The trip to Chippenham paid off and, in a small way, contributed to the benefit of the breed. Mr T W Williams, Caerynwch, also sold many stock bulls out of him, which made their mark on many herds within the breed. One of the earliest sons to be sold out of him was CAERYNWCH ERDDYN 2nd, which threw excellent stock for Mr John Vaughan and Alun, his son, of Moel Iwrch. The most notable grandson of PENYWERN SERAFF 18th was IWRCH SERAFF 2nd, who, in turn, sired such notable bulls as NEUADD DAFYDD DDU 168th and NEUADD DDEWID 68th, out of the famous Neuadd herd of H M Jenkins and Son, Neuadd yr Ynys. Both Neuadd bulls won championships at the RWAS at Llanelwedd, but they were the more valuable as good quality stock getters at the Iwrch and Fodlas herds, where they produced many good young bulls. Another bull to throw its stamp on the breed was FOEL MYRDDIN 16th, who was used extensively in the Seisiog and Graig Goch herds. Many good bulls and females out of him have been shown and sold by Mr Goronwy Jones and his son, Emyr.

Talking about shows reminds me of an amusing episode that happened at the United Counties show while Mr Bennett Jenkins, Cerrig y Trane, was judging. He invariably sported a large thumb stick and, before the start of the judging, with the help of this stick he managed to discover a hole in the ground in the middle of the ring. He duly probed the hole with his stick and discovered it was rather deep. When the steward got hold of the stick and pushed it into the ground, it disappeared down the hole. He put his arm into the hole, to retrieve the stick, and failed completely. Judging was due to start and the hole was made safe by plugging with a post, to which a Welsh Black sign was affixed. After the judging was finished the steward suggested obtaining the services of a JCB to rescue the stick but, eventually, he took off his coat, stretched down through an enlarged aperture at the top of the hole, and the stick was retrieved. The hole was probably caused by a tent pole hole used at a previous event.

That story brings to mind the time when Bennett Jenkins was fencing on top of a hedge bank and his employee suddenly realised that he had lost his knife. Bennett searched him thoroughly and scoured all around. In the end, Bennett concluded that the knife could only be in one place and he ordered the employee to remove the newly inserted fence posts. As he predicted, the knife was found down in one of the post holes.

Apart from our successes at home, we benefited greatly, and still do, from Gwilym Edwards's initiative in expanding further afield. We have members in Germany, the Old Commonwealth, in Scotland and in England. We are now at a stage where Scotland and Canada, in particular, have a big contribution to make in a forward movement of the utmost importance. Our cattle have overtaken other regional, local breeds; they lend themselves to development along different lines and are wonderful at adapting to various climatic and geographical conditions. They are on the road to the international recognition they deserve and all the commercial advantages which accrue from it.

I remember once negotiating with a certain farmer, a Welsh Black breeder, for the purchase of a particularly outstanding bull. This coincided with a trip to Scotland that had been arranged for a party of Welsh Black breeders. During its route up through North Wales the coach had to stop at traffic lights opposite the field where the bull was grazing. Most of the eager breeders rushed to the windows to admire the bull, while I sat in my seat, cold shivers rushing down by spine, cowering in the background, trying to ignore the bull on which my heart was set. All was well in the end because I clinched the deal on my return and acquired the bull to add to my herd.

Without such broad expansion and the creation of new focal points to generate new bloodlines our genetic base would have shrunk to danger-point, especially once the best breeders came more conspicuously to the fore, not least through modern processes of selection. The whole thing might well have ended up as a farce played out by a handful of eccentrics.

Dai Davies travelled indefatigably, even to places where little had been accomplished, and there was, to begin with, scant hope of concerted progress. In part because of the distances involved, the Cinderella of the regions was the English one but he would visit shows and other venues, regardless of the paucity of any immediate return, and he encouraged regular contributions to the Journal from the English section. How much of this endeavour was appreciated in the heartland which stumped up most of his wages I would not like to guess. However, very slowly there came success, and the English Section now has the appreciation it deserves. We have even enjoyed the Presidency of one of their officials.

The arrival of technology for the objective assessment of breeding values by the measurement and comparison of heritable traits brought the need for a leader of special qualities to head the Society. The Meat and Livestock Commission instituted Young Bull testing stations at Holme Lacey, in Herefordshire, and at Ingliston, near Edinburgh; it supported co-operative breeding, as well as on-farm assessments; much later, BLUP.

For MLC Wales Welsh Blacks were the focal point of all this, and a further boost in the use of new technology in selective breeding came from the Welsh academic bodies of various kinds. The Department of Agriculture at Bangor started the Haulfryn co-operative breeding scheme with a nucleus with 19 members who contributed top stock against an entitlement to draw replenishments from the scheme. Aberystwyth University started a Welsh Back herd; and Welsh Blacks were kept for experimental breeding purposes at the hill station at Pwllpeiran and at IGER, the grassland and conservation establishment at Aberystwyth. All this activity happened without any real competition from other beef breeds in Wales. Its value to the Welsh Blacks, even if measured in terms of the publicity alone, was tremendous.

The backbone, on-farm procedure, with subsequent selection of the best candidates for

Holme Lacey was secured by an arrangement in which MLC involved the Society and the University, on very favourable financial terms to participating members. After some initial response the arrangement began to peter out, despite unceasing exhortations to keep it going, from Brinley Davies, the Welsh MLC beef expert, who also published calculations of its benefits. However convincing the figures, they were published in vain as far as the scheme was concerned.

Perhaps it was just too much, too soon. Progress of this kind requires a very long view and some practical adaptation. It would mean translating a deep sense of tradition into long-term strategies of a forward-facing kind. The Council adopted a neutral stance, at best, and Dai Davies also took this position. There was no one with the vision or the necessary influence, to say nothing of a willingness to accept unpopularity, to create the impact which would be needed to keep up the impetus.

There might also have been some lack of diplomacy on the part of MLC. The mysteries of computer technology tended to be presented by this body as some impenetrable hocus-pocus which the layman was expected to take on trust. One cannot detect any indication of them admitting of a role for the practised eye of which breeders are justly proud. This was the breeders' own mystique. The computer makes no allowance, either, for the expert's built-in evaluation of mothering and associated traits. Finally, to expect the upland suckler cow to flourish on a gulp of fresh air and a drink of cold water, like the ramblers, would surely be the asking too much even of that all-embracing, obliging, adaptable animal.

Although the uptake of the scheme was less than widespread, some very good stock was infused, via the pedigree market, from Haulfryn and its members, from the large undertakings like Tyddewi, in Pembrokeshire, and Shanno, in Scotland, and from some other individuals, too. In this way the venture made a contribution at the highest level, which would otherwise have been restricted to show winners and the fame attached to prominent breeders of long standing.

Slowly, Welsh Black beef qualities came to the fore. At Smithfield successes rose and rose, increasing steadily towards the day when Welsh Blacks were Best Native Beef Breed exhibits.

I should apologise to my readers for rushing ahead by quite a number of years but my object is to relate my own experience of the breed as well as my impressions of trends and attitudes as they developed. This rather long period includes a time when I had my own herd but had not, as yet, developed my numbers to a level consistent with such activities as those I am describing. As for my attitude then, it may have been one of curiosity rather than conviction. I should add that, much later, I became a member of the BLUP recording Elite Club, and am actively concerned with co-operative recorded breeding and selection of stock for semen collection and embryo recovery.

In the earlier stages of Dai Davies's tenure, at any rate, the owners of large established herds were prosperous and it was they who kept the breed in the forefront of people's minds, above all through participation in competitive classes at agricultural shows. Without these exhibitors the Society would have been in dire straits.

Showing, while it is time-consuming and expensive, offers each breeder a personal shop window and the prospect of an immediate sales advantage. There was, though, a tendency for the same herds to appear all the time, perhaps, because showing is a skill which has to be learnt. The Society's publicity associated with these events was largely in the hands of dedicated members. Dai Davies must have been a master of diplomacy to co-ordinate them all. They were tremendous individuals, some of them showmen in their own right, all prodigious workers, and a few were also extremely generous.

In the beginning there was a publicity caravanette, which did the rounds of shows until it became hopelessly prone to breakdowns. After that the publicity machine went through a series of movable pavilions, then, a marquee, and, finally, it saw the creation of our excellent, permanent clubhouse at the Royal Welsh show ground, now expanded to embrace a Society office and our new marketing lounge; my personal brainchild, this.

If you want to promote Welsh Black beef you have to cook it; so there were barbecues. If you want to give the public a longer look at the stock than they can get round the show ring you have to mount special demonstrations. These were always imaginative, with people there who were qualified to speak about the exhibits, and they proved to be outstanding in every way.

The originator of the demonstrations was an old man of great vision, amazing energy and a rare gift of natural kindness. Every chance meeting with him, even just a brief conversation, would leave you feeling somehow befriended. E. L. Jones, affectionately known to us all as E. L., was born on a farm in Herefordshire, became a brilliant academic and, finally, Livestock Officer to the Welsh Department of Agriculture at Aberystwyth University. He learnt to appreciate the Welsh Black breed so much that, on retirement, he devoted all his energies to the Society. For the demonstrations he travelled endlessly, to select the stock; he persuaded breeders to contribute and prepare the exhibits; devised the format for each different venue, and, of course, was present all the time, at half a dozen shows, every year. A member of Council and of the Publicity Committee, E. L. Jones was the best Society President we never had.

His strong views, expressed on some occasions without the slightest equivocation, came *ex-cathedra* and never failed to create a stir. He was, at first, quite sceptical of MLC for he suspected, not without reason, that they nurtured a tendency to roll up all their data into a single, hence meaningless, index in which some important traits of the breed might be sidelined. I well remember the first open meeting, held to inaugurate the Haulfryn Scheme, when he lost his cool completely in making just such an accusation. He went over the top, nobody quite knows why, and the scheme, as it developed, paid close attention to female traits. A few years later, in 1984, he broke the mould when he was judge at the Royal Welsh Show. When the judging was finished he held a post-mortem during which he laid emphasis on the characteristics to look for, or else avoid. Giving reasons, he picked out aspects like locomotion, which might not otherwise get too much attention. He also attacked the tendency to make show animals over-fat. Only E. L. could say these things and only he could get them across so that they would not be forgotten. He even committed the ultimate heresy against the razzmatazz tendency of the show circuit when he recommended that there should be show classes for groups consisting entirely of cow-families.

He was the conscience of WB members; he had a way of addressing anyone he met as 'young man', but whether he impressed the really young ones as much as he impressed those of my own generation is not easy to tell. His epitaph is something of a mystery, too, since I have not been able to trace its source.

L.

The corn was Orient and immortal wheat,
Which never should be reaped, nor was
ever sown. I thought it had stood from
everlasting to everlasting.

It is difficult to assess and appreciate all the work that somehow gets done. I refer, as an example, to the three members who carried out all the inspections for the Super Cow scheme, running into hundreds over very many years, and applying the same standards all the time, to put into effect a scheme which Edwards had initiated in 1959, to supersede the original Register of Merit, which had been solely concerned with milk Yields. Such dedication is hard to credit when one come to write it down in retrospect.

Senior amongst them was E. H. Williams, whom I was fortunate to know well. He built up a foremost herd, Penywern, which contributed many an outstanding animal to the breed. His PENYWERN SERAFF 18 was invaluable to me when I had started my own herd. E. H. Williams's farm, which he had bought from those Morrises who famously supplied the original heifer which presented my uncle Richard with triplets, is not far from Ynys, the home of my uncle's herd. Throughout the years when I was slogging it out milking but always hoping to start my own herd of Welsh Blacks, E. H. Williams gave me friendship and understanding. It was friends like the Williams family who helped me to maintain my contact with the breed and gain a growing insight and a degree of objectivity over such a long time.

CHAPTER SEVEN
Working in Co-operation

All told, I had milked cows for thirty years, since I was eighteen. Although my father was seriously injured, he was on hand for about six years to help me with advice and guidance. He died in 1954 and then the responsibility for managing Brysgaga was entirely mine.

Milking, and especially the gradual conversion to Friesians, was not where my heart was. Indeed, I remained closely involved with my uncle Richard's Ynys herd right up to his death in 1961. Meanwhile, I got on with making a living.

Luck came my way when I was able to buy Brysgaga from its new owners, the University. As it turned out, it was easy. Finding the money was not nearly so easy. Another thing which does not come cheap is land improvement. There are subsidies to be had for this but they are hedged about with conditions and provisions, and the problem of accommodating stock in the meantime is no small one. Brysgaga has some beautiful bottom land but there is not much of it. Higher up is a plateau of great potential but it is wet and it used to be near-useless scrub. Now, it is productive.

I am not a single-species farmer. My sheep enterprise is as important to me as the rest; hence the pressing need for useable acreage. Even what I could improve and make use of at Brysgaga would be nowhere near enough for an appreciable venture into suckler beef. To achieve this took me another twenty years, when I bought Pantycarne, a farm above Llanilar, some seven miles away.

During the post war years, every autumn, I visited many farms to procure ewes for breeding. On one occasion, accompanied by a young child, I went to inspect ewes in the Ponterwyd area. After clinching the deal we were invited into the house for a cup of tea. As soon as we stepped inside the door a sheep dog, that was chained to the stair banister, rushed at us and but for the length of the chain would have bitten our legs off. Once seated round the table we were offered the choice of a home-made apple tart, a thick yellow one at that, or a shop-produced current cake. Having earlier seen the tart being prepared on the table, with the cats assembled thereon and their hair intermingled with the pastry, I hastily opted for the *cacen siop* (shop cake). The young lad, in his innocence, decided on the tart. Nevertheless, I bought ewes there for many years as they did well, coming off a healthy place.

I also bought ewes from another farmer for many years and had occasion to visit this farm to buy a stock trailer. It transpired that they had had a nasty accident with the trailer. While towing it behind the Land Rover, with an Aga cooker in the back, it started swinging and the driver failed to control it. It subsequently overturned and the old boy in the front hit his bald head on the kerb of the pavement. Later, while negotiating a price for this trailer, the owners said they were desperate to get rid of it but, even so, they stuck out for a price that was hardly less than the cost of a new one. Remembering my previous dealings with them, I eventually bought the trailer, although I would probably have been better off buying a new one. It must have been easier to buy the sheep.

A prominent sheep farmer who had many ewes always said that a sheep's greatest enemy was another sheep, and then he added, 'plus netting.' In the 2001 crisis one could have added, 'Foot and mouth, too.' His sheep had always been used to roaming about at will, before the advent of netting.

Whenever I think of sheep sales, it brings one memory that makes me smile. It happened at the Devil's Bridge Auction Mart, where Mr. Arnold Rees was doing his best to enliven a slow day. He started to auction some ewes for a Miss Humphreys of Dolgors and, in spite of his best efforts, the price crept up to £2 a head. Arnold Rees looked hopefully at Miss Humphreys, who shook her head, so Arnold had another try and after a long struggle managed to get a bid for £2-2s.

"Selling now, Miss Humphreys," Arnold said.

"Certainly not," she said.

"You better had, Miss Humphreys," Arnold told her, "it's your old friend Mr. Vernon Howells who is bidding." He accepted the bid and concluded the deal. Now, Miss Humphreys," he said, probably feeling rather pleased with himself, "how about a bit of luck for Mr. Howells. In fact," he quipped, "what about a bit of love-making?"

Miss Humphreys turned on him in a flash and retorted loudly enough for all to hear, "He'd better be quicker with his love-making than he was with his bidding." It brought the house down.

One of our neighbours used to enjoy driving his tractor to do field work, and when harrowing or ploughing he would sing at the top of his voice and could be heard for miles around. Another of my neighbours, who could hear this singing very plainly, when it was good weather for hay-baling, would always say, "The baler is singing as well as that fellow over there."

I had always belonged to Brysgaga, where I spent my entire childhood, but it is hard to describe my intensified sense of belonging when the cherished homestead came into my ownership. I have seen this feeling manifested in others who managed to buy their farms and can share with them the same inward joy which I experienced. My joy was enhanced by my marriage to Dorothy in 1959. I fell utterly in love. Considering my inexperience and that I thought of nothing other than my consuming passion, I was very, very lucky. It is also the one piece of good fortune which has lasted a lifetime, through all sorts of weather, foul included.

The day came when Dorothy was to bear our first child and I came to visit her in the maternity ward shortly after Rowland was born. On the way along the corridor, I caught up with a bachelor friend. He was carrying a bouquet of flowers and, out of curiosity, I asked him whom he was visiting.

"My wife-to-be," he replied, and hurried on.

I went to the ward where Dorothy was and peeped through the window at my new baby son.

"You can't deny being the father of this one, Mr. Rees," said the matron, and I had to agree with her.

Dorothy had a good laugh when I told her about our bachelor friend, who, I am happy to relate, married the lady, she has been a good wife to him and they have been happily married for many years now.

What better could we do for the old homestead than to direct our energies towards making it beautiful. Dorothy planted the flowers. I planted the trees at the entrance to the farm, to recall the original name of the place, Agam's Wood. The flowers decorate the approach to the house, and

are the pride of Dorothy's magnificent garden. I tidied up the drive, diverted a brook which used to threaten the house, addressed myself to a row of old barns, to make them attractive, and Dorothy embarked on what would become a life's dedication, to develop the house and bring out all its ancient glory.

She did all the hard work herself, but it takes a special talent, a profound knowledge of antiques and an unfailing spatial eye to make a success of such a project. By the time we retired and left Brysgaga, which we did on the occasion of our son Rowland's marriage, she had created something precious to hand on to the next generation. She managed all this while bringing up our two children, Rowland and Mary; and helping on the farm if needed. Finally, Dorothy has always supported me in all my business, connected first, with Welsh Quality Lamb and then with the Welsh Black Cattle Society.

From the outset we both played our part in the village. Its character had already begun to change by the time we married. The first impetus for this was, undoubtedly, the withdrawal of the erstwhile influence of the Pryse family. There were physical signs of this waning influence: for instance, the little Ysgoldy Lady Pryse was not re-established in its original form; it became, instead, the headquarters and changing room of the Bow Street Football Club. The whole atmosphere of the area changed, as well. Lady Pryse, now consigned to a smaller holding, still dominated church services, rather like a symbolic flagpole; but no portrait of a paternalistic figure commanded mantelpieces under a gathering film of dust. The original tenants bought their farms and the *gwerin* began to prosper as self-respecting wage-earners.

The television-age had begun. It opened up a whole new world of images, ideas, tastes and aspirations. The village now had mains electricity, water, and sewerage. There was an expansion of employment as the Plant Breeding Station (later IGER) grew into an institution of international repute. The old days of cow/pig/six hens installed in the yards of some of the cottages had all but disappeared.

Bow Street was still a settlement extending from the railway station over three linear hamlets. We still had parish councils, forerunners of the community councils of the present day. As elsewhere, the seats on ours, Tirymynach, were occupied by those who were willing to serve. Like chapel elders, they were not elected in any but an assumed sense. Such a system was bound to make for continuity: only like-minded people were invited to participate. Parish Council affairs were less moribund than one might suppose because the character of the issues dealt with began to change as time went on.

In 1963 I was invited to serve on the Parish Council, young as I was. I came into local government at a time when considerable developments were afoot and much of their success, or otherwise, would depend on the stance adopted by our local council. There was a need for further housing, yet the last thing we needed was

more in-filling of gaps left in what was already a ribbon village with elements of back-filling. We started with a social housing development at the Lovesgrove, or southern, end and reaching over two cross-avenues, with an old-folks' home as an integral part. We now have further social housing, at the other end of the village, and several private developments, running off the main road in both directions. We also have a large, compact development on the Clarach road. All told, there is well laid-out housing supporting some 1,500 people.

All this was achieved, not always easily, but we all knew what was wanted and, especially, what we needed to avoid. Over a few commercial projects our objectives did not always find unanimous approval, which was where the residents became involved, with petitions and site meetings, at which they were able to air their views. We now have a busy, thriving community with amenities that are the envy of some of our neighbouring villages. Elected we were not; but no one could quibble at our democratic procedures.

There were also schemes pushed through at our own initiative. We had to overcome considerable obstacles connected with the site which we earmarked for our new, purpose-built school. The land was sold to us willingly, but the provision of adequate drainage put a number of snags in our way. If we were unable to overcome them, no one else would. As for the old Rhydypennau Primary School, it is now a centre for the pre-school infants. Quite a few thoughts go through my mind when I collect my grandson from this seat of early learning.

At the other end of the spectrum, we have self-contained flats for older people, mentioned elsewhere, as well as some small units for the same purpose, rarely with any vacancies, because of the contentment and longevity enjoyed by the occupants.

What really pull village life together are the projects which have little to do with council activities and to which people contribute not only funds, although it must be said that we have collected thousands of pounds from local residents, but physical effort as well. The important one is our village hall, which went through many changes since starting life as an old YMCA hut, bought in Pembrokeshire and condemned by the chapel elders as too frivolous. There have been major and minor objectives over the years, one of which I recall with a smile, was when we went to buy two second-hand snooker tables for the youngsters, and had to manhandle them out of the YMCA premises in Chalybeate Street, Aberystwyth, where they were, and fetch them home to Bow Street.

There had been three tables at the YMCA; they were seldom used, due to lack of space, and they were to be sold by auction. I went along with three friends to see what we could get. There was already a bidder for the first of the three and he seemed to be bidding rather high. We wondered whether we would be able to afford the other two

as the bids continued to rise. Eventually, that first table went under the hammer. We did not realise that this was an antique that would soon be on its way to America and the bidder would go, rejoicing, to the bank with his profit.

I bid successfully and paid £30 for one table, £40 for the other, and a little extra for the scoreboard, balls, cues and triangle frames. That was the start of my headache, however. Snooker tables have slate beds under the green baize, and each slate weighs between four and five hundredweight, or 200 to 250 kilos. My friends and I had brought a lorry with us, to carry our trophies home, but first, they had to be dismantled and put aboard. Ifor Owen, who was an ex RAF pilot, knew a thing or two about this kind of job and, under his guidance, we made slings out of hessian sugar beet sacks, and managed to carry the slate blocks out without damaging them. Ifor put the tables together again once we reached the hall. It took the equivalent of a day's work to set them up again, and I was glad that my companions had been strong men, or we should never have managed it.

I remembered this in 2002, while I watched the final of the British Open Snooker Competition Final taking place between Welshman, Mark Williams, and Irishman, Ken Doherty. Terry Griffiths was one of the commentators. Ken Doherty suddenly missed an easy black, just when he seemed to be on his way to making a substantial break. Terry exclaimed, 'Duw! Duw! He's missed the black,' thus reminding us that he was also a Welshman.

Of the minor things we do regularly, are things such as arranging the stage, collecting chairs and tables and preparing the place for various events. Everything we needed to make fullest use of the hall we now had. To see it today, anyone would think it had been purpose-built. Everything happens in that hall. We bring and we buy, we exhibit endlessly; we meet, on an ever-larger range of topics, and we even rise to holding our concerts, too. The hope is, of course, that we can interest the many incomers in these activities, to try to get more social cohesion into the village. Such things do not happen overnight but the beginnings are there.

Our crowning glory is our fully-fledged football stadium. I have described elsewhere how we played on all sorts of fields, even one with a tree on the touch-line, and changed before and after matches wherever we could. Now that we have such excellent facilities, I sometimes have to pinch myself when I attend our business meetings. Bow Street F. C. has always had a good team, and still has. Something which occupies our minds even yet is the effort to maintain a junior team. This is of the utmost importance, not merely for the sake of training young hopefuls for the Bow Street Magpies and not just to keep youngsters off the streets. Especially with a mixed Anglo-Welsh population and with youngsters attending different, mainly language-based, secondary schools, it is vital that we create a sense of local belonging. This applies not just to the youngsters, either; this kind

of thing is impossible without the active help of the parents. The Community Council has not, of course, a direct remit in this respect, although it supplies an element of cohesion which would otherwise be lacking.

On the subject of the football club, The Magpies (*Y Pïod*), and the contributions made by the local people, I should like to mention one man in particular, David Emlyn Rees. In 2002, Emlyn, President of the Bow Street Football Club, was awarded a Long Service Medal of Distinction by the Central Wales F. A. Emlyn served the club for something in excess of fifty years, and I was asked to make the speech at his presentation night. Emlyn began as a goalkeeper and, when his playing days were finished, he continued to help and support the club. It was his impetus that saw the club acquire its present day pitch and amenities, and every person hearing of his award said how richly deserved it was. Bow Street has always been fortunate in having so many people dedicated to the welfare of their neighbours, and Emlyn's contribution is just one example.

Emlyn was, on one occasion, keeping goal and a penalty was awarded to the opposing team. Emlyn waited until the penalty-taker from the visiting team had lined himself up and was poised to strike, when he lifted his hands to indicate that he was not ready. He removed his false teeth and placed them safely, in his cap, on the grass beside the goal, then signalled that he was ready for the penalty to be taken, by which time the poor fellow had lost his grip, blasted the ball and it flew high in the air, way over the bar. This episode has gone down in local soccer legend as one of the best confidence tricks and it has often been related in the years thereafter.

Not so many years ago, one Mr Tom Hughes was the manager of Bow Street FC, and he used to relate how he beat one reputable team by bluffing them with tactics. Instead of operating the 4.4.2 formation, or the 4.3.3, he confused them by playing the old fashioned outside right, inside right, centre forward, inside left and outside left formation. By so doing, he boasted, the opposition was so confused that Bow Street beat them all ends up.

Referring to another former Bow Street manager, I recall how he inferred that many potential players residing in Bow Street were playing for other clubs outside the village. Somebody named two such players, who were twins.

'Well, yes,' he said 'but they're *odd* anyway.'

In 1966 I was elected to the Rural District Council. This was a different council environment, with different problems, and one thing I valued especially was that its territory covered the whole of North Ceredigion, the home of so many of my uncle's fellow breeders. I knew the area well and I served on the RDC until it was disbanded in the local government reorganisation of 1974. It had a much wider remit than the old Parish and Community Councils. It was also one which turned up jobs which one would least expect to find. One was the RDC's support for Emlyn

Tanner's pony-trekking establishment, on Forestry Commission land at Bryngolau, above Penrhyncoch. Pony-trekking was not the streamlined industry it is today. It was breaking new ground and its success was far from assured. No one could see me as a man with a passion for horses but this venture fired my enthusiasm. I contributed a few ponies, and my family went trekking, with much enjoyment: Dorothy and the children went along and they were joined by the family of Cyrus Evans, the Clerk to the RDC, and others. I even allowed myself to be pressed into leading some of the treks, regardless of my utter inability to cope with a mount bolting off with its rider, and other, luckily harmless, emergencies. It was amateurish, yes, but the atmosphere was marvellous and all the participants had fun.

Give or take a rough-hewn beginning to his enterprise, Emlyn Tanner was conscientious and his venture basically well organised. The Forestry Commission appreciated this and were supportive. Soon, their support assumed a more solid character: Emlyn was already employed by them as a vermin exterminator and now they assisted with the expansion of the small pack of foxhounds he kept, and with investment in purpose-built kennels for the Penllwyn and District Fox Destruction Society. This has nothing to do with riding to hounds for sport, where the chase concludes with the hounds tearing the fox limb-from-limb and in which anyone who can ride a horse can participate, without possessing any relevant skills whatever. To these huntsmen, there is no contest, therefore no sport, and the adrenaline aroused engenders nothing more than a barbaric blood-lust.

Our own hunt goes out on foot, with guns, on Saturdays given up by the members for the purpose of getting rid of the foxes, which are a menace to their stock. The hounds are there to get the foxes running, for the guns to dispose of. The bag amounts to a considerable number of foxes; we would not give up whole Saturdays for less. When Emlyn Tanner's health gave way and he retired, the kennels were relocated. The guns still go out. Times are harder now, there is less employed labour on farms and farmers are finding it more difficult to give up whole Saturdays. If there are not enough guns, the hunt becomes less effective, but the need is as great as ever.

There cannot be a stock-farmer anywhere, down to the humblest small-holder, who has not, at some time, had the horrifying experience of foxes killing his chickens, or his lambs, sometimes even in his presence. One of my uncles once lost fifty lambs to the fox, all in one season. I have myself witnessed a vixen taking a lamb as I approached a lambing enclosure. Her stealth was so consummate that even my excellent Blue Merle bitch failed to notice. I chased her away, unfortunately with the lamb she had just taken, leaving the ewe bleating hopelessly for her offspring. I was witness to the same thing, years later, right beside the house at Brysgaga.

The sense of outrage, pain and bereavement is hard to convey. It may be a natural act on the part of the fox but the suffering it causes to the animals in our care is what matters to us. This is something our Animal Rights friends will never appreciate, for they know nothing about animals and cannot see the difference between the cruelty of hunting with dogs for pleasure, and doing it humanely, with guns, to remove a verminous threat to other animals.

This reminds me of an animal story that happened one sunny afternoon, on the Promenade at Aberystwyth, towards the end of September. There was a 7-seater Mitsubishi 4 x 4 parked near the pier in an area where parking was limited to two hours. Inside the vehicle was a lovely, excitable, Cairn terrier. A female traffic warden came along and when she noticed the little dog., she walked round the vehicle, several times, and then decided to telephone and share her discovery with another eager beaver, a lady from the RSPCA, who arrived on the scene quite soon thereafter. Both women seemed as excitable as the little dog, and the RSPCA lady also circled round the vehicle a few times. This, of course, attracted the attention of passers-by, who also came up to have a look, causing the little dog to become even more excited.

After a while, the owners returned, all six of them, grandparents, parents and two children, the youngest of these in a push-chair propelled by grandpa. The back door of the 4 x 4 was opened, the little doggy popped out, and, none the worse for wear, enjoyed a bowl of water. Confrontation was imminent, and young dad led the doggy away, on its lead, after snatching the paper from the windscreen and depositing it in the nearest litter bin. Both traffic warden and RSPCA lady continued their aggressive confrontation with the other people, the warden writing furiously in her little book. Young dad and doggy returned from their stroll, the whole family went on board safely and grandpa drove slowly away. According to the name on the back of the vehicle, it was bought from a garage in St. Albans. It was very intriguing to watch, but I am sure those people will think twice before spending another holiday in Aberystwyth,

To return to elections; I have mentioned that there were no such things as formal elections in the early days of our local council. You served if you were acceptable to the other members and did not arouse fierce opposition from the rest of the population. It meant, of course, that there was little chance of great changes in policy, which could only occur as the older members faded out with the slow passage of time. Nevertheless, old men do adapt to changing circumstances and it would be unfair to say that they opposed new ideas. This undemocratic state of affairs came to an end. Local government became a target for political parties, and elections were contested at every opportunity. I decided I would not go that way, and continued to stand as an Independent, thus depriving myself of the backup of a party machine, which was at the disposal of my rivals. I was secure at local level but could do nothing to defend myself against detailed and organised

canvassing for the new County elections, for a body which later replaced the old Rural District Councils.

The party machines were up to every technical and tactical trick in the book, which the electors found confusing. After the event, people who had inadvertently lent themselves to such ruses could be quite upset. In my opinion, there must be something wrong with a system which enables candidates for election to go breezing in to a farmer's kitchen, suggesting they are engaged in a minor formality, without honestly apprising the busy man of the importance of the endorsement he is being invited to make. One example of this type of behaviour concerned a situation where one of my sponsors had signed another sponsorship form after completing mine and after being assured it didn't matter. Thereby, I was disqualified because my rival, aware of the duplicity, delivered his form to the Town Hall ahead of me. Practices of this kind can only bring the democratic process into disrepute.

For me, there was no time to spare for disappointment. I continued to serve on the Community Council, as it is now called, and still do. But I was drawn more and more into the co-operative marketing of sheep and, then, cattle as well. Like all these extra tasks, it was not particularly onerous at the beginning but it became so demanding as time went on, that I really do not know how Dorothy and Rowland made room for it all, to say nothing of Trefor, our faithful friend and servant.

I must make proper mention of Trefor. At RWAS in 1983, he was presented with the 40-year Long Service Medal by the Queen herself, who attended the show in that year. It was a great occasion for him and no less so for us, as it gave us all an opportunity to reflect on those long years we had been together. As a live-in servant, Trefor never lost the demeanour of the old retainer, though his mindset lay well above that of the simple souls I have described elsewhere. You could trust him with anything you gave him to do and you would know, too, that if you failed to get home when you were expected, he would quietly get on with what needed to be done, through all those milking years, especially. Trefor was a man of few words; his was a silent kind of understanding. He deserves all the affection and gratitude with which I remember him.

This is where I confess to taking a liberty, yet again: that of extending the story well beyond the point in 1978 where I was able to fulfil my ambition of changing from dairying to stock-breeding and which marked the end of the interim period I set out to describe in this chapter.

CHAPTER EIGHT
Time to Realise that Ambition

Co-operative marketing has appealed to me from an early stage. First, it avoids a situation where it is every man for himself, each exposed to competition from other small producers and played off against each other by a concentration of buying power. Second, there is no obvious connection between the ability to produce good stock and selling it. It is a fact of life that some people can sell, others not. Selling costs time and money.

Finally, co-operation, as an ethos binding farmers together in their chosen profession, is something which has stimulated my enthusiasm ever since I witnessed it in my early youth. At that time it was driven by necessity. Those upland farmers, above Glandyfi, with their thousands of sheep and no mechanisation whatever, could not have survived at all without pooling their resources to do all those seasonal jobs. And then, that cluster of famous cattle breeders, lower down, could scarcely have managed their business without mutual help. It gave rise to a culture of mutual trust and common decency.

All this may sound as if I were a bit starry-eyed.

I was to discover, much later, in another context, that collaboration, when it comes to voluntary blood-line input, can be somewhat reluctant. I have to admit that, except at times of crisis, a vital ingredient of successful co-operation is a recognisable identity of common interest. More to the point, one valid criticism of co-operative marketing is the fact that, where there is a body committed to taking any or all of a member's output, the need to think ahead and seek to provide what the market requires tends to be of secondary consideration. In a broader context, such things are of comparatively limited importance when compared to the enormous advantages, especially in a modern commercial setting. Recently, my optimism seems to have been vindicated by the readiness of so many farmers to contribute, even in hard times, to provide match-funding towards obtaining a grant for a Welsh Black Beef Marketing Group.

My younger readers will feel rather as if I am bombarding them with a whole jumbled alphabet of acronyms, unless I try to explain briefly the various bodies involved in agricultural marketing and technical development. We started when everything was on a wartime footing, with all control in the hands of the Ministry of Agriculture, MAFF, to whom all our output was sold at pre-set prices. They spawned the Fat-Stock Marketing Commission, FMC, in part with co-operative characteristics. It employed field-men and graders, who undertook the grading of stock at markets, and selection on farms, for onward sale at auction markets, with animals on the hoof, or to go to abattoirs, again, on the hoof. The men employed by FMC were of amazing calibre, especially considering the number of people involved. The field-men were usually small farmers working for an additional income which was by no means generous and they became indefatigable travellers. They were trusted, and deservedly so. With very rare exceptions, they never abused the opportunities which undoubtedly presented themselves at a private level. The graders were trained operatives. They were absolutely impartial, perhaps they had to be, with all those farmers watching their verdict on every animal. Certainly, the return on lambs jumped enormously as soon as FMC took over.

ADAS was involved more broadly with Agricultural Development and had a finger in all manner of pies. Marketing was one but it also amassed a whole army of technical advisers. These covered everything in which one could conceivably engage. More specifically concerned with technicalities of animal husbandry but not

directly with marketing is MLC, the Meat and Livestock Commission. Additionally, at a purely voluntary level, there are the National Farmers' Union, NFU, and the Farmers' Union of Wales, FUW.

What made the difference, though, in terms of marketing, was the addition of the Welsh Agricultural Organisation Society, WAOS, part funded by London but run regionally by local officials and local committee members. I sat on this body for a long time. It has had a few remarkable officials from the outset, who gave it both expertise and dedication, who set it on its policy-path but who always had their feet on the ground. The right man at the right time was Alun Thomas, who quickly became the Central Council Officer for Wales. He used all available administrative and financial ties to London and went on to succeed the late Elwyn Thomas as Director of WAOS, until his retirement and succession by the Chief Accountant, Don Thomas.

To co-ordinate centralised selling, which was the immediate part of the remit, he was careful to collect an excellent sales-team, Glyn Williams and David Evans especially. They were genuine experts in their field. To facilitate the formation of marketing co-operatives a body of administrators was formed. They were closely tied to London, where grants for this purpose were individually vetted and determined, and even more so when they became the regional protagonists of Food from Britain. By definition, such people are keen to justify their existence and most of them nursed a degree of ambition to push things along, perhaps a little faster than the client might wish to go.

The idea of co-operation extended to agricultural merchandise of all descriptions. Our farmers' co-operatives were members of the Federation of Agricultural Co-operative Societies, but this was a large, overarching organisation which offered little advice, guidance, or any other help.

By the time WAOS arrived on the scene, several co-operative ventures were in dire straits. The biggest and the one with the most intractable problems was Cardiganshire Farmers, based in Aberystwyth. I was on both committees and know that, without the help of WAOS, and especially its commercial consultancy services, it would have been difficult, if not impossible, to pull Cardiganshire Farmers' Co-operative round. It is now a successful mini-conglomerate with branches within reasonable distance of one another and a sensible central depot.

Co-operative marketing of livestock began quite early, and on a rather *ad hoc* basis to begin with. The earliest stirrings came in the form of pig-weaner groups, facilitated by FMC, their reason for existence being to place weaner pigs with farmers wishing to take them to market-ready weights, for sale through FMC.

Next came the marketing of lambs. The formation of groups proceeded apace, on a county basis, beginning with Carmarthen and, by 1970, had expanded to groups in all Welsh counties. WAOS co-ordinated all this and initiated the establishment of Welsh Quality Lambs Ltd., WQL, as well as a subsidiary, Welsh Store Stock, for store-cattle and store-lambs.

I was WQL's chairman from its inception to its demise in 1986. It became part of my life, inevitably, in view of the effort it needed, but especially because I saw in it the fulfilment of my ideal of farmer co-operation. I feel that my attitude to this venture was rightly held, considering the fact that the lamb prices overall which were realised by its members were 3p/kg above the English average.

At a personal level, there was an irony inherent in all this work that I was doing for co-operatives. In my own business affairs I am nothing if not cautious. I slogged it out milking cows for two decades, until I was ready to change. Time was to show, however, that I chaired an organisation which became the victim of its own success. I suppose it is axiomatic that whoever is in front cries, 'Back,' and those behind cry, 'Forward'. These latter ones will carry the day until trouble comes, when the rescue attempt falls to the ones in front.

Like so many well-conceived and thoroughly-executed schemes, WQL began by going forward in leaps and bounds and was well able to generate finance for its own expansion. Beyond that, however, we still lived in a period when there were no sources of investment for smaller businesses, apart from the banks, whose policy was essentially one of short-term lending. The time came, inevitably, when we were faced with the opportunity to take a quantum leap ahead, using the only means available, or risk being overtaken by competitors. There are times when luck and good management seem inseparable. WQL started as a procurement organisation and worked on a commission basis, placing members' stock with wholesalers. It was a 2-tier organisation, marketing centrally on behalf of all the county procurement groups.

Its success was due in no small measure to Bill Metcalf. He left to join MLC, and his place was taken by a thorough-going meat specialist, Harold Oliver, who was instrumental in setting up our operation at our first abattoir, with John Meade as manager, at Builth Wells. This was an abattoir which we bought from Midland Shires Farmers. It was quite small and by no means handled all our stock. So, with two strings to our bow, we had the best of both worlds.

If WAOS was our fairy godmother, its magic wand could take the shape of a stock-prod with a gentle current at its extremity. We bought another slaughterhouse, in North Wales; then Marchwiel, which was ideally located to take large numbers of small lambs off the hills; and, finally, Henllan, near Denbigh, which was mainly geared to beef. That meant that we had acquired three new abattoirs in a very short time but we still had no capacity of a standard suitable to handle meat for the export trade.

Midland Shires Farmers, also a co-operative and a competitor, whose slaughtering side was now in low water, approached WQL with a proposal for a partnership in their export-standard operation at Craven Arms, only a short way across the border with England. Then, MSF retrenched even further and passed us their share at a nominal figure. Also involved in this business was their sale to us, on very favourable terms, of their abattoir in Welshpool, which we closed. We sold this asset, as well as some property and some land, to try to reduce our financial exposure, but meeting the export standard required at Craven Arms was extremely expensive and even an excellent new manager on the site, Philip Webber, who joined us with specialised experience gained in Devon, was unable to turn it into a profitable operation.

We had burnt our fingers, like MSF before us. Worse than that, the man who had managed Craven Arms went into partnership in another abattoir, at Nantmel. It was a major upset. Given WQL's successful track record in every other direction, most outsiders might think it would be possible to come to an accommodation with the bank and get back on the road to recovery, which is exactly what MSF had done. But that would leave out of account that small, elusive thing called market sentiment, otherwise known as the Lemming Instinct for self-destruction.

The pride of WAOS, WQL, had enjoyed a glittering press. I had been our-man-in-Brussels, where I went to represent the interests of Welsh producers. Harold Oliver and I were photographed at official receptions, cutting an anniversary cake, and receiving a prestigious business award. When the mighty fall, there is an awful splash, and waves, too, which ripple endlessly.

First, John Meade grew restless at the Builth abattoir and moved into partnership with Philip Webber, to set up an operation at Eardisley; which meant two good men gone at once and into competition at very close quarters. Then, there was the other new abattoir at Nantmel, also within shouting distance of Craven Arms. This was followed, inevitably, by nervousness at the bank and they started pressing just when some flexibility would have helped. It got to the stage where they put us into intensive care, raking in horrendous fees in the process, for the work of their *in-situ* representatives.

The only hope for our survival was to get as much throughput as possible. I appealed to members to put in stock, mainly cattle. They responded well. I put in a very large consignment at what I hoped would be a crucial moment to tip the scale. It did, but not as I had anticipated. I had hoped that a large input would boost our turnover, give a swing, and a healthier look to our overdraft and thereby help to turn the corner. That was the moment when the bank pulled the plug.

All those who had responded with a big effort became non preferential creditors, and we all know what that means. My own huge loss was one thing; those sustained by others were different. I did not expect them to be forgiving and they were not. My reputation was flat on its face. I might have reached rock-bottom but there was a wonderful bedrock. This was Dorothy, who was

indomitable. I could not have gone to pieces, even if I'd wanted to. It was one of those times when you make a new and precious discovery. As I took stock of what had happened and thought back on what I had done, I found other consolations were there, too.

For the benefit of my younger readers, I should explain that bankruptcy in the late nineteen-eighties, and in an environment like ours especially, was more than simply the material loss it is today. It was a disgrace, deserving of every possible show of humiliation, not necessarily entirely in private. I think back on Mr Frank Wright, a dapper little gentleman with white hair, who farmed in Norfolk, who used to come regularly to Wales to buy his Welsh Black cows in order to eat and clear the carrot tops which were grown on 1000 acres and sold under contract to Sainsbury's Supermarket. He used to relate how he started from humble beginnings, with only one cow, and how he used to carry the milk cans from house to house. Eventually, he made enough money to buy another cow and sell more milk but it became too much of a burden and he bought a pony and cart to carry the milk. Along came a hard winter and he lost his pony and one of his cows died. So he was back to square one. He made enough money to buy a few chickens and he sold the eggs. His field was on rent and he managed in time to rent another field, living all the time in a tiny chicken shed. Slowly he expanded until, in his later years, he farmed 7,000 acres, including 1,000 acres of carrots. This I consider to be a fabulous example of going from rags to riches.

Whatever else happened, these were the circumstances which taught you who your friends were. For me, these true friends were my fellow breeders of long standing. Already a member of the Council of the Welsh Blacks, I was president-elect less than a decade later. It might have been easy to suppose that, following the WQL débâcle, my public life was at an end; it was just beginning. WQL had been in existence for sixteen years, from 1970 until 1986.

However time-consuming it had been, my involvement with WQL had not taken priority over everything else. My Welsh Blacks were now established as a closed herd and were the fulfilment of a dream of so many years. As for co-operation, I have not been cured of that enthusiasm. In the area of co-operative breeding and the marketing of Welsh Black beef I am pushing for more participation, all the time. However, I still regret what happened to WQL. We need it now, more than we ever did. With the benefit of hindsight, it might have been better to remain a procurement agency entirely. I came to this conclusion too late, as so often happens, but it was a great lesson, nonetheless.

CHAPTER NINE
Expansion and Development

The year was 1976, I was already in my 46th year, still milking Friesians for a living and edging forward to the one thing which had been my goal since childhood: Welsh Black cattle. The time was ripe and I had to think carefully about the options before me.

The Milk Marketing Board was still committed to collecting all the milk which its members produced. That had a major disadvantage, in that we were obliged to sell to this one outlet. There were now so many very small milk producers, that the costs of collection were escalating, to say nothing of more modern handling/holding requirements. It was a time when there was an over-supply of milk and this surplus production necessitated a change of strategy from the Board and the Ministry of Agriculture, who were considering offering an incentive to go out of milk, which would apply to more than just the very small producers. This came on top of EEC legislation to do with the Common Agricultural Policy.

It was evident that most of those producers ceasing milk production would enter the livestock-rearing sector, and in order to maintain their previous level of business activity they would need to increase their land-holding to accommodate a less intensive type of husbandry. The acquisition of more land was something which had been part of my own plans ever since I had nursed my ambition to change to Welsh Blacks but now I would not be alone in searching for further acreage. I knew that there was little point in sitting back and hoping for something to come to me and I set about seeing what was likely to become available.

My search started with Evan Lloyd, who had been a farmhand at Brysgaga when the tenancy was held by the Thomases, the immediate predecessors of my father. Evan Lloyd was now in his eighties and he worked with his son, Dewi. Between them they produced very well regarded draft ewes for the farmers' markets.

The Lloyds had a sheep-walk at Bwlchygarreg,

above Talybont, in the foothills of Plynlimon, which is the highest in the immediate area; hence the demand for their sheep, which would thrive on lower ground. In addition, they owned a farm of 115 acres, set quite high up above Llanilar and about seven miles from me. This farm was also devoted wholly to sheep. To say these were men of the old school would be an under-statement, if their way of life were to be the measure. In commerce, however, they knew exactly how to build a reputation on the basis of their advantages, stick to what they were doing, and make money slowly, over many years.

I had bought draft ewes from them regularly and reckoned that I had come to know them well by the time Dewi considered selling Pantycarne, his holding at New Cross, and above Llanilar. His wife hailed from somewhere away, no one seemed to know exactly where, and was now said to be feeling homesick. Possibly, she was suffering from exhaustion, for she had, by this time, presented Dewi with a whole row of twins, all as unruly as she herself was erratic. The likelihood was that Dewi might have to pack up and go with her, back to her original home.

This is the kind of news that travels fast in rural areas, and Dewi had approaches from a number of people who were interested in buying his farm but with each prospective purchaser he went through endless Stop/Go sequences while savouring the experience of making a hard sell, and, each time, pushed them all right up to the wire before changing his mind. Even Dewi saw that this ploy could be overdone, when it reached the stage where no one would take him seriously. This realisation dawned, it seems, just at the point where other hopefuls had gone away disappointed and the field was wide open for me to buy not only the property but 300 ewes as well.

In view of the increasing demand for land and having this opportunity for the taking, I felt resigned to the fact that I would have to pay somewhat over the odds for the extra land I knew I would have to buy to fulfil my purpose. Whatever other upsets there might have been in my life, that turned out not to be one of them. All things considered, Pantycarne came at a reasonable price. The rest of the exercise was pure farce.

The big day came when I went up to the sheep walk at Talybont with my quiet, no-nonsense stockman, Trefor, to pick out our 300 ewes. We had been told that they would all be penned for our inspection, and so they were, in an impressive, big shed of a size seldom seen as high up as that. As the proceedings got under way, the atmosphere became so strange that we began to feel that anything could happen. The sheep were fine. The trouble lay in a crowd of unmanageable children, who were supposedly on hand to help but were predictable only to the extent that they never restrained any sheep escaping from the compound and persisted in ignoring all instructions.

Trefor and I were shocked. This was not an age when children were deliberately irresponsible; indeed, we had an example of the converse right opposite Brysgaga, at Ruel, on the hill across the valley at Bow Street. Here was another enormous family, and each time they moved their sheep to and from what are now the IGER experimental plots, every conceivable gateway, opening or other hazard was covered by a child and the whole exercise would proceed like clockwork, to the satisfaction of the children themselves.

As for the Lloyd brood, they contributed one thing they seemed to be proud of, and that was an astonishing vocabulary of the most insalubrious kind. Finally, I rather think because everyone had had enough, children, father and grandfather, someone shouted, 'Stop,' when we had picked out 200 ewes. Nothing would induce them to carry on to the next hundred. Despite any previous arrangements I might have made, I had to be content with 200 ewes. I thought I had seen a few things in my time; I was amazed; Trefor was shattered.

We were not finished yet. Pantycarne has a main house, of fairly recent construction, and a couple of small cottages converted from the original farmhouse. This was where there were tenants, students. 'I should hang on to those,' Dewi advised, assuring me that they were OK, they kept an eye on the stock, etc.

Remembering the episode with the children up at the sheep walk, I might have guessed that Dewi's idea of reliable people would be a touch eccentric, and so it transpired. Within days of my taking over Pantycarne, the students' domicile was raided by the police and various substances taken away. Mushrooms, the so-called magic kind, were illustrated on wall-charts, and, deep in the woods, there was a nice plantation of cannabis plants. At this time there was a whole rash of hippy/junkie students drifting about the Llanilar/Tregaron area, forming a community of sorts. It was a fair bet that, where there were a few, there would soon be more.

I went to talk to them but their attitude was not co-operative. It seemed unlikely that they would change either their behaviour or their occupation of what was now my property. That was not good enough for me and I sought advice from a friend who is a very eminent lawyer. From him I learnt that a criminal charge of possession of an illegal substance was sufficient to cancel any tenancy entitlement the students might have had. As it happened, this was a lucky outcome for me but while it was in progress, it was, to use their own expression, hairy enough. It was just one of the things that had to be dealt with before I was able at last to get back to the purpose of my acquisition: farming.

I had walked Pantycarne and thought that there was more water underfoot than might be expected. One can always find a possible cause for that sort of thing. It turned out that this excessive moisture was due to a whole series of leaks in a mains pipe which crossed the land. Land used to carry stock needs good fences; Dewi had renewed a few of them at Pantycarne but certainly not all, which left me with another job to do. In spite of the setbacks, overall, this was a happy acquisition and I have never regretted it, even in later years, and even after buying land much closer to home within two years of my purchase of Pantycarne.

In the time that I have been compiling these memoirs, I was reminded of my rather fraught negotiations with Ifan Lloyd, and eventual establishment at Pantycarne, when I took a walk on the mountain with Gwilym Jenkins. Ifan Lloyd was born in Blaenclettwrfach, above Caerglwyddes, Talybont. At that time there were families living at Blaen Clettwrfawr, Esgairfoelddu and Blaenclettwrfach, a cluster of little farms on a small patch of mountainside. We met one of Gwilym's workmen, busy on a long stretch of dry-stone wall, alone with nature and seemingly content with his lot. I asked Gwilym where the three farmhouses had stood and he pointed out to me three piles of stone, all that remains of homes where large families were reared on a minimal income.

When I thought back over the years, I saw here a clear illustration of how great has been the extent of rural depopulation. Gone are those days when shepherding scattered flocks of mountain sheep and tilling a walled patch of acid soil for a few vegetables were sufficient to support the occupants of these now derelict homes, and how simple were the demands of those families, living on their meagre incomes and a tradition of self-help. It was no wonder to me that Ifan Lloyd was a hard man, with his background of poverty and harsh upbringing. He was a hardy man, too, who was able to walk great flocks of sheep all the way from Bwlchygarreg down to Pantycarne. He was a thoughtful man and when I spoke to him of the future, he said that however he developed, the land was always diminishing before the stock.

By now, it was 1977. The additional land I needed for the new enterprise was ready, waiting, with sheep on it, temporarily. After those adventures with Dewi, his offspring, and the junkie tenants, a return to more conventional ways of doing business was welcome. This was the subsidised disposal of my milking herd under the milk-outgoer scheme. What followed was the realisation of the purpose I had cherished all those years. I had been so intent on this, that, looking back, it seems amazing that nothing went seriously adrift with my best-laid plans. I will attribute this to the fact that I gave it a lot of careful thought, even if I admit to having an element of luck. I hope this book will also be read by younger breeders, or perhaps even those who have yet to make a beginning. To them I can only say that, with this breed, it can be done, without tears and even by the uninitiated.

Welsh Blacks are not a particularly numerous breed. They are exceptionally well documented. We have had a succession of good administrators, who have seen to it that pedigree certificates mean what they say. There is a lot of material, such as well-laid-out herd books and good breed journals with excellent articles and illustrations, better, I am proud to say, than those of most other breed societies. The Welsh Black breed is represented at shows big and small, and both sorts of shows are useful; and the Welsh Black demonstrations are worth a very careful look. Anyone who wants to learn about the breed is assured of help on a generous scale from breeders and officials alike. What the intending breeder needs to bring to the job is application, lots of it.

I had followed both the breed developments and the changing fortunes of the society as time went on. There was movement in the field of performance testing but it was not over-popular amongst established breeders, who had managed very well without it and were apprehensive lest their traditions be undermined. It would not be a difficulty for me until I had several generations of breeding to underpin whatever was to be monitored.

There had been near-disaster when livestock prices crashed, in 1974. It was followed by a slow recovery of prices and confidence. New herds had been started, but these had not yet reached a stage where they were being sold as production stock at the Society's markets. This was still firmly in the hands of the old-established breeders in the Welsh Black heartland.

It was a world which had not changed much since my youth, but the way in which I made my start was different from what I had observed being done by others. I deliberately avoided a slow build-up by a process of buying and selling of females. As far as I could see, this could easily become a habit. It was very tempting, however, at a time of prolonged and roaring inflation, when there was money to be made on a constant turnover of stock.

To build a stable herd was my objective from the beginning. I covered many miles, looking at Welsh Blacks and at their related stock; and many evenings were spent comparing pedigrees, until the great day arrived, in January 1979, when I went out with money to buy.

There were New Year sales at Dolgellau, the weather outlook was atrocious and transportation difficult. I watched the weather deteriorating as the second sale day wore on, preoccupied with thoughts of carrying my precious stock through the treacherous pass over Cader Idris, through a hollow-with-bends alongside the Tal-y-Llyn lake, and up a steep incline towards Corris. I had driven lorries before and managed to extract them from an assortment of tight spots, but that had been some years ago now. Things had gone so well at the sale and I wondered whether my luck would hold until I got home.

The incline leading towards Corris was covered in wet snow on ice and there was a whole line of cars behind me. I had the best chance of all of making progress, with all that weight on board, but I didn't stop to consider the situation. I put my foot down, in desperation rather than in hope, and up we went, with no hesitation at all, the whole line of cars following in my tracks. I do not remember the rest of that journey, and by the time I got my animals unloaded I was too exhausted to appreciate the good fortune of that eventful day. It had been an outstandingly good mart, the first one to be extended over two days, and it worked in my favour.

I had bought all the females I wanted, from the FOEL, DYSYNNI, PENYWERN, RHYDGARNEDD, PIGAU, HARLECH, CAERBELLAN and CADER herds. I had followed my favourite criteria but the most important criterion was milkiness. Although I had purchased nothing from NEUADD, I had inspected the bull I wanted, SEISIOG PRINCE III, prior to the sale, and this bull had plenty of NEUADD blood.

I had made a start, with nine maiden heifers and SEISIOG PRINCE III. I added to my herd the last of the TYHEN cows, purchased from a remarkable family of two aged brothers and two sisters, all of them unmarried, who had a telephone but no other facilities and where a visit would take all day. They were such unusual people and so dear to me, that I could not let them retire without buying something. As it happened, the cow was a worthy example of their excellent stock. In 1982, I bought CHWAEN SALLY II at the Chwaen Goch reduction sale, and VAUN ADA with her heifer calf, VAUN INKY, at the Vaun dispersal sale at Kerry. Then, I closed my herd. For the benefit of those who might not understand what closing a herd means, it signifies purchasing no further females. All the new blood comes in through bought-in males, but the dam-lines continue through generations of progeny.

The established nomenclature of pedigree animals follows well-defined rules. The breeder has a chosen prefix, mine is BRYSGAGA. This is followed by the name of the dam, and the female progeny takes its number in the sequence of that family. Thus, BRYSGAGA MARI VI is the daughter of BRYSGAGA MARI V. In the case of male progeny, these, likewise, follow the name of the sire, with the appropriate number, e.g. BRYSGAGA BLEDDYN XXXI, even though the original BLEDDYN may have been bought in from another herd.

Some of my readers might be interested to know which bulls I brought in after SEISIOG PRINCE III, using the same selection methods as previously. I had a friend who used to say that buying a stock bull was like buying a pig in a poke, and if you wanted to know what you were getting you'd better breed him yourself. There is some truth in that, but it would take a large herd to achieve it without breeding too close. Also, if you knew what you were doing, the poke could contain a very good pig indeed. It is a fact that the period I am considering produced three really outstanding Welsh Black bulls, which left their mark through some generations: CHWAEN MAJOR XV, NEUADD CAWR XXXIII, and PENYWERN SERAFF XVIII.

When the latter was for sale, the same friend went berserk at the end of the telephone, anxious to make sure that I really would dispatch my son Rowland to buy him next day. It had all been arranged, anyway; and what Seraff did for my herd might have been difficult to equal with the narrower choices imposed by my own breeding. In later years, when I had more scope and was increasingly involved with our Welsh Black joint

Brysgaga Seraff 26th

breeding programme, I was able to use some of my own bulls to good effect.

Thinking about that frantic telephone conversation reminds me that it was not only humans who could go berserk. It was in 1989, at the Royal Welsh Show, when I had trouble with my show heifer, BRYSGAGA NERYS. It was a scorching hot day, and poor Nerys went berserk simply because she was unable to tolerate the heat in the cattle shed. She was not the only animal to suffer, and exhibitors, including me, had to keep washing them with water, to cool them. The water was pumped to the site from the river and treated with chlorine. The drinking water had to be left to stand in the buckets until the chlorine had subsided, otherwise the cattle would refuse to

Mr. John Rees and his wife, Dorothy, showing Welsh Blacks at Pwllheli Show, 1992

drink it because the chlorine went into their nostrils.

The bulls I added, to follow SEISIOG PRINCE III, were DOLDOWLOD JIM V, RHYDGARNEDD BANNER XVI and, then, PENYWERN SERAFF XVIII himself; followed later by CHAKA EDWARD X, a grandson of the famous CHWAEN MAJOR XV, LLANDRE LLEWELLYN, and, finally, YSGUBORIAU BLEDDYN XIII, my Royal Show winner of

Ysguboriau Bleddyn 13th, United Counties, 12th August, 1993

1992, which were in addition to the bulls of my own breeding which I used myself. That makes a total of seven bought-in bulls, over a very long period, that extended to the end of the nineteen-eighties.

Not one bull was bought on the spur of the moment, and of the later ones especially, each has many a story attaching to the history of the Welsh Black breed. The years which culminated in the purchase of Seraff were the foundation years of the herd and the ones which cast the mould for the later and quite different developments which were to follow.

From a business point of view, there is a big difference between relying on a monthly milk cheque and starting with a group of maiden heifers whose progeny would take at least three years to get to market if, indeed, they were to be seen as production stock, that is males, or females, of not-quite first-class order, or families, which needed to be thinned out to balance up the herd. At the same time, the inflationary boom of the nineteen-seventies was coming to an end.

I had more sheep now, producing more finished lambs each year, but even this was another, if smaller, waiting game. I bought one Charollais ewe-lamb and patiently sat tight until I had a whole flock, related to the one female. Prices for imported sheep were artificially high and this was the time when other people were turning over quick money in the scramble. My policy was to select for good birth-coats, for poor ones indicate a weakness in the breed, and wait until I had sufficient terminal sires to service my Welsh Half-bred ewes and gain the value which attaches to this kind of integration. I never regarded the sheep as value-added and they were never put into shows.

Once I had potential winners to come out with, the cattle soon revived my old passion. SEISIOG PRINCE did me proud and so did PIGAU EIRLYS VI. It was a joy to be back in the old, familiar atmosphere, now as a participant in my own right. Furthermore, I was beginning to get females accepted into the Society's Super Cow Register, in increasing numbers as time went on. The importance of a place on this register cannot be over emphasised. It was not long before I was elected to the Council of the Society, membership of which was dominated by my old friends from the original Welsh Black heartland. At the end of the nineteen-eighties my cattle prices were rising and so was my confidence.

CHAPTER TEN
The Stony Path to Exports

Until I came to write this account I had reflected little on the circumstances surrounding the early years during which the foundations of my herd were laid. At the time it was a privilege to be accepted so quickly into the world in which I moved. I was also extremely busy. Welsh Quality Lambs made so many demands on my time, that I often wished I had more hours in the day.

To start with, I suppose I took Welsh Blacks more or less as I found them, or had expected to find them. My herd had its beginnings in the period which looked back to the Edwards era, a sort of golden age whose forward vision was still only vaguely appreciated. The importance of the big, enterprising Scottish herds as a means of enlarging the breed's genetic base; the development of the Welsh Black female into a larger, more suitable beef dam, and her management to meet modern conditions; the realisation of the Welsh Black's competitive potential, on a par with other beef breeds, were all things, despite persistent pleas from Brinley Davies

of the Welsh MLC, which were perceived as concepts on a distant horizon.

There was a deep faith in the uniqueness of the breed and an innate fear of the danger of sacrificing much if the Welsh Black were to be reduced to the level of a conventional beef breed. I should quote from the valedictory article written at his retirement by our secretary, Dai Davies, who had refrained, over his tenure of 21 years, from any kind of comment on wider issues. What he had feared concerning developments in the second half of the seventies and beyond was that the influx of Continental beef breeds would see us reduced, not to the level of a conventional beef breed, but to that of a supplier of suckler cows for the up-and-coming crossing herds; with prices and future prospects permanently depressed to match. My own entry into the breed came at the beginning of this period.

Since then, I have experienced the transformation of the breed to the very thing conventional wisdom had dreaded. We saw the emergence of the Welsh Black as a beef breed able to compete successfully with the performance of imported as well as British breeds. To put this another way: it was a transformation from a suckler-cow breed with a beef dimension to a beef breed with a suckler-cow dimension. The possession of an additional dimension, either way, is the very thing which helps the breed as it is today to be kept pure and used in closed-herd situations and to be adapted to a variety of climates and systems of husbandry.

Currently, I feel we are in danger of being bogged down by paperwork and not enough fieldwork is performed. I quote from Page 93 of the Annual Report of 1970, written by G Williams Edwards after he had served for 20 years as Secretary of the Society.

"Most of my work as Secretary will be devoted to outdoor work, visiting farms and giving after sales service. What members want is good service and good prices for their cattle." We could do with better advertising of our sales at this moment in time. Looking to the future, we must ask ourselves where we're going. We are still too absorbed in self-interest and short termism. We have to stop deceiving people with FAT and blown up hairstyles. Improving conformation and performance and developing markets must have prime emphasis. We have a breed, which is synonymous with eating quality, but we are still fragmented selling the same product in competition with each other.

The issue of our journal in which Dai Davies announces his retirement is also the last to carry a contribution from Brinley Davies, our indefatigable advocate of modern technology as a means to improvement. He also has his axe to grind. Welsh Black breeders were reluctant to participate, he says, on the grounds that their breed was different. That is another way of expressing our extra dimension. It would be a pity if it became a bar to progress.

More and more members entered the new Animal Health Scheme. Mainly, this covered three prevalent diseases, of which EBL was seen as the most important and the most dangerous. As things turned out, it probably did not merit the importance ascribed to it when it was discovered in some imported cattle, which was at about the same time as Maedi Visna was diagnosed in sheep. However, the Health Scheme arising from it was an excellent concept. In addition to blood testing, it involved a degree of on-farm discipline which was good for all of us. It made everyone more aware of herd-health, as distinct from single-animal treatment, and enabled us to cope with other diseases, such as Johne's, at a later stage.

As for interest in technology, this had declined by the end of my first decade as a breeder, if, indeed, there had ever been much enthusiasm, anyway. One important development which affected this aspect of farming was the emergence of embryo technology. This was taken up by Haulfryn and great hopes for it were expressed. Whether for lack of facilities, or because a degree of secrecy must always surround this kind of research, a whole raft of commercial firms came

Brysgaga Brenin 44th, selected for semen collection under 5b Scheme, 1998

out with their own procedures, which proved superior to the rather homespun efforts at Haulfryn. They were clearly unable to compete in this very vital field and slowly the whole undertaking went towards its demise and a final dispersal sale, some years later.

This did nothing to recommend the concept as a whole. It played straight into the hands of MLC's detractors, just at a time when it should have been obvious that fertilised embryos for export would enjoy a greater demand if, like those produced by other beef breeds, they could benefit from the backup of objective performance data. There were alternatives available: the Beef-breeder Scheme offered a broad-ranging evaluation of commercial production factors in addition to on-farm weighing, with appraisal of contemporary comparison.

Hindsight is a wonderful thing but, looking back on all these suspicions and animosities, one could wish that someone had come out with some kind of slogan, or a few short, sharp sentences, to inspire us. There were breeders who had been established very much longer than I had, whose aloofness was a matter of choice, not circumstances; meanwhile, for me, it was a subject of interest, not involvement. I was not yet in their league. However, I am certain that, at the time, I did not make the link between objective performance data as a stimulant to exports in competition with other breeds, and the effect which exports, in turn, could bring to bear to raise our pedigree prices in the home market, until, some time later, exports to Germany suddenly took off. The effect on our domestic price-levels was immediate.

As time went on, some interesting figures appeared and the lack of publicity they received was a pity. For instance, MLC used the available figures to establish beyond doubt that, far from being slow to finish, Welsh Blacks were at least as fast as Herefords and much leaner at the crucial 400-day stage. In the absence of real interest, these things were not discussed as widely as they should have been. What brought about a very gradual change in attitudes was the undisputed rise in the general standards of our stock.

PENYWERN SERAFF XVIII, one of three bulls reckoned to be outstanding in their time, was followed by others, whose fame may have spread less widely, but which had all it took to continue to raise the profile of my herd still further. CHAKA EDWARD X was one of these. I later sold him on and, when last heard of, he was still going strong. LLANDRE LLEWELLYN gave me many an excellent stock bull; and RHYDGARNEDD BANNER XVI was later sold to Colonel Williams Wynne, who exported him to Germany. All these bulls would, at an earlier time, have been regarded as exceptional but there were other breeders besides me who were working with other herds which had the same capacity for progress.

BRYSGAGA BLEDDYN 44 was approved for semen collection and his semen proved to be very popular and was widely used. He was a bull full of character, of great strength and with a good back-end. He was used in the Maescastell herd for many years, and is now with Mr. & Mrs. Beynon, owners of the Tyddewi herd. Both these people are amongst the foremost breeders.

In the last analysis, it is all about prices, although saying this does not make me so mercenary as it might seem. There have been many sales which have given me satisfaction, pleasure, and even friendship. There are always opportunities for follow-up of the animals and their performance in their new surroundings. If they do well it is a source of pride, but there are times when something you sell to someone can be the start of real progress somewhere and your satisfaction at being involved is more important than you might have imagined.

I once sold a few heifers to a couple who lived on a smallholding in the Cwmgwaun Valley. Mr. and Mrs. Phillips had no big ideas but, in their hands, my heifers did exceptionally well. That is where it all started. They bought a bull from me, which they brought on tremendously. By bad luck, the bull suffered an accident, which meant he could not be shown but his successor still did well. The Phillipses went on to top the points league for success at smaller shows, and, on more than one occasion, came very high in the South Wales herd competition. More recently, they won the HSBC trophy for the BLUP-participating herd with the steepest improvement curve. They hoped to continue to do well. Their serious entry into Welsh Blacks has meant a lot to them, and their friendship means very much to me. There are many occasions, not so dramatic as this, where the cattle will serve to introduce you to people who become your friends and with whom you can share your ideas and experience. It is sad to relate that Mr. Phillips had his leg amputated in the summer of 2002 and because of this his involvement with breeding and showing will probably be curtailed. He is an inspiration to us all.

Apart from the fact that RHYDGARNEDD

BANNER XVI was later exported to Germany, there were Welsh Blacks in the Old Commonwealth as well, where they had been for quite some time. Progress there was slow, and each country, with a different climate and ecology, wanted a different kind of Welsh Black. Nobody got rich but the great and the good undertook many journeys and the publicity was, and still is, a fillip to the breed.

I had greater hopes of Germany. The distances were manageable, ordinary farmers could visit us and see the stock at our shows, without too much trouble; and we could assess their needs more easily. I visited Germany twice myself, to good effect; and, years later, mine was one of two herds visited by a group of German breeders. The amusing part of that was, that the pub close to Brysgaga had just recently changed its name from The Black Lion to The Welsh Black, and this seemed to impress our visitors more even than the cattle! 'E. L.' told me, years ago, that animal health would become more important in years to come. How true his words turned out to be.

Sadly, BSE came along to put a stop to all of this. We had, it is true, laid the foundations for later developments in the export of semen and embryos. If we had made waves with our exports, our presentations at agricultural shows were excellent. I have described elsewhere how Malcolm Richards and E. L. Jones, in their different ways, dominated our show publicity and did so with dedication, generosity, and imagination. There were the big shows, the Royal, the Royal Highland, Great Yorkshire and, of course, our own Royal Welsh but this was also a decade when the smaller shows went forward by leaps and bounds. They had always catered for everybody, crafts included. There were now additional incentives: profitability and, above all, local reputation.

All our Welsh show grounds are worth a second look. Some are in such beautiful, natural settings that this alone would be enough to make a visit into a good day out for local residents and tourists alike. There they will discover upgraded amusements for children, more sophisticated craft marquees and, a major attraction, the horses. Horsemanship became more competitive and more widely popular as the decade went by and all our little shows had a piece of the action. It was not just the riding, either. There are the ever-spectacular draft horses, something out of a different world altogether; elegant ladies in driving competitions; and our own, home-grown speciality, the Welsh cobs. At small shows they were always run and were always good for some excitement.

I hope that this stirring entertainment does not turn the livestock, which is the real reason for such shows, into a sort of side-line for a few persistent enthusiasts. The breed societies started awarding points for rosettes at designated shows, in some cases just for attendance; and the smaller the show, the better the chance of picking up those titbits of glory. Every little helps to get a breeder in line for his herd-of-the-year, flock-of-the-year, or

whatever else is to be won. Some people will travel unbelievable distances, to quite small shows, for just this purpose. Whatever their motives, they did a lot of good by promoting quality stock ever more widely. Where the sheep were concerned, however, I wonder whether all this pot-hunting tended to defeat the purpose of the village show, if the competition was just between small flocks established in the immediate area. Even the standard of preparation became so professional that the average small farmer had trouble finding the time, to say nothing of the skills; only to have his entries ignored by a judge looking for the likely prize-winners or, worse, flock-masters known to him.

A lady I knew, who once did a small judging job, was so exercised about this problem of favouritism, that she determined to spend the same amount of time on every entry, however poor, and then made sure that each flock went home with a rosette, for being placed fourth, fifth, and so on. One may protest but, at the end of the day, she was thanked by two small flock owners for the attention she had given to their sheep, which had made their participation worthwhile for the first time ever. Who knows, she might also have given encouragement to some beginner with genuine potential.

Our Welsh Blacks had a points system, too. But there was more to it than that: specialists apart, our native breed had its own aura of glamour for the public at large. Their beauty came conspicuously into its own where the cattle lines were in the open and showed their glorious black coats resplendent in the sunlight. One has no need to be a son of the soil to appreciate that. As the decade went forward, more professionalism came into the judging. The Society asserted its presence at all the shows. We established a panel of judges, although nothing would ever inhibit that favourite spectator-sport of criticising the judges' decisions.

There is a two-way advantage with the presentation of good stock at shows. It lifts the image of the breed and it satisfies the breeder. By now, times were more commercial and the sheer love of the atmosphere and companionship gave way to the need to create a shop window for one's own name. No one can put a figure on what that may have done for individual prices. The show was still an environment where each visitor had his own ideas, all dependent more on his eye than any other considerations, as his strictures on the judges could demonstrate.

It helped to have Welsh Blacks everywhere, of course, but, overall, the Society designated fifteen shows, running from June to late August, which carried importance towards points for various prizes. By the time my son, Rowland, and his wife, Janice, set out on their summer-long tour of the shows, it was not little, homespun, village affairs they were visiting, and the competitions they entered were of a very high standard, where every point counted.

We had seen the influx of imported beef breeds and, for obvious reasons, their breed associations were just as eager to obtain classes at as many

shows as possible. Some of these imported animals were sensational, especially Charollais, and Blondes d'Aquitaine of immense proportions. There were some which remained novelties but still attracted attention, as well as the commercially viable ones like the Limousins, which were seen initially as a direct challenge to British Herefords rather than our Welsh Blacks. It made the Hereford breeders get their act together in very short order, too hastily, some might say, but an extra sense of urgency might have helped us, too, if we had seen ourselves as direct competitors at an earlier stage. However, it stimulated in us a renewed emphasis on beef quality; i.e. we recognised the source of profitability and laid a special stress on our status as a British breed. Our Winter Fair at Llanelwedd had been a popular venue ever since we had our permanent show ground and facilities there. Now, our entries got better and more numerous; participation, though, is not a cheap exercise.

Even more demanding is Smithfield, in London. For years we had put our cattle in, for very scant return. Then, we became recognised as a British breed. We started inching forward; in the fullness of time we would even win the top prize.

In the meantime, there is somebody I want to mention. A compliment is due to the late Queen Mother. She has been praised for her breeding of racehorses and her other extravagant hobbies but in her interest in British-bred agricultural animals she was unique. I have looked in vain in her obituaries for mention of this. At the Royal Welsh you could see her crest in the trailer park, and her

North Country Cheviot sheep, unobtrusive, in the sheep lines. At Smithfield, there was evidence that she was interested in British cattle. No other luminaries showed this genuine support, which was an encouragement to us, especially while we were still fighting our way up, even more than when the great moment came, in 1992, to receive the Queen's Cup from her hand. This tribute is from me, a Welshman, one who tries to value encouragement from all interested quarters. I refer, also, to our Patron, HRH the Prince of Wales. Prince Charles takes enormous trouble to serve the Society. His enthusiasm for all things organic is not one I would share without some reservations but it means a great deal to him and he pursues his objective with dedication and sincerity.

During this time, my children were growing up. Mary, my daughter, was showing a distinct bent for art and design, and Rowland decided he wanted to study agriculture. Even if there is a strong family tradition and you have, after all, done it yourself; there can be moments of uncertainty if your son decides to follow you into your own line of business. You ask yourself a hundred times whether this is what he really wants, or whether it just happens to be there. In Rowland's case there was no possible doubt. It may seem far-fetched to think it was in his genes, rather than in the conditioning he had undoubtedly received as he grew up, but there was no denying his intention.

It is a joy, of course, to make a discovery of that kind. But it is an additional responsibility, too.

Would I now have an even longer view? Would I be equal to accepting that he would not see everything the way I did; that he would have to look forward to different times and different circumstances? Would I learn to develop a set of assumptions which would have a new and different perspective? Awareness of such things became part of my thinking, that much is certain, and, though I had lost my own father at an age when there could be no perceptible generation differences, I only had to look around me to see father/son relationships working out, or otherwise, in all sorts of ways. The land and an attachment to it, can be the cause of an awful lot of tears.

None of these things arose. The days were too full; too many things were happening. For one thing, we had bought more land, in 1979. This was some 30 acres, running down along Tyn Rhos Lane, the next one to Cross Street, nearer to Talybont, and right down to the main A487 road. It was fertile and extremely well-watered; protected from drought by its northerly aspect.

Much later, more of this land would also come our way but, for the time being, the piece we were lucky to get had plenty of hard work waiting for Rowland, Trefor, and me. Then, Rowland was still a student and, I hope, I respected his many personal claims on his time. This land had charms all of its own.

The time would inevitably come when Rowland would be domiciled at Brysgaga and Dorothy and I would want to retire to an attractive environment, which would not be too

Author's son Rowland Rees showing Ysguboriau Bleddyn 13th as Champion at Denbigh & Flint Show, 1993

far away. My readers will have seen that I have a habit of initiating some things in very good time and will not, therefore, be surprised to learn that I put in a planning application for a bungalow on this land. There were objections to the application but I do not give up easily. After twelve years of hassle, to say nothing of bloody-mindedness on both sides, I had my way.

There were many calls on my time; especially while Rowland was still a student and Trefor was

Brysgaga Brenin 36th, Champion Bull, Llandovery, Autumn 1994

going gently into retirement, with most of his time spent working at Pantycarne. Welsh Quality Lambs had come to an end, as had my days in local government but, as a member of the Council of the Welsh Blacks, and one of the younger ones at that, I found more and more responsibility coming my way. My herd was now showing the fruits of the work of those early years, it was advancing to a leading position, with demand and prices rising all the time. Above all, my cow numbers were rising, too; so that, even when Rowland was able to join me, we were engaged in a great deal of work. The work you cherish is never a treadmill but it gets nowhere unless you can organise it properly.

I have referred to this period as a decade; in reality it lasted longer, possibly to the end of the tenure of Dai Davies, our Secretary, and the arrival of Evelyn Jones to take his place, which coincided with many new departures in which I became involved and sometimes played an initiating role. All this was despite the fact that Brysgaga was still a very young herd compared with the old-established ones to which it was now offering serious competition. It was a position which needed to be consolidated. In commercial terms, that meant going with the flow, using the shows as a shop window, not just to satisfy that old urge, but to win as many important trophies as would enhance the name sufficiently to make it memorable in the sale-ring. The effort to keep my prices moving steadily up was no small one and I pursued it to the exclusion of everything else.

I would dearly have liked to win the Royal Welsh, in addition to the Royal at Stoneleigh, but was prevented from entering my sure winner by an anomaly created by a rule forbidding the entry of any animal with connections to the judge at that show. Much later, I did have the best Group of Three in that show, which was not quite all I had hoped for, but you can't win them all.

Something else exciting was happening, too. In 1991, Rowland married Janice, our lovely young daughter-in-law, a farmer's daughter from Maesycrugiau. It meant, of course, that we had yet further plans to make, for there would be two families now, and two households, and, perhaps in time, a new generation

When Rowland and Janice spent an entire summer going round all the shows, and one has to be young to have that much enthusiasm, the result was a colossal board full of rosettes. We still have it. Because this series of journeys was so protracted, it required an exercise in logistics, which paid off, and I think it was fun as well. Our prices rocketed again. It was something we needed; and later events would show how badly we needed to do all these things when we did. I observed all this with pride. It was Rowland, my son, who was presenting the cattle, winning all those rosettes. His role was not that of a dogs-body, somewhere in the background, while his father collected the honours. He was seen to function independently and to know exactly what he was doing.

Before expanding on the new phase in the nineties, I will let the personal aspect of that period end with a marvellous, heady summer, and with a move by Dorothy and me to a bungalow a couple of miles from Brysgaga.

CHAPTER ELEVEN
Opportunities

The first half of the nineteen-nineties was dominated by the arrival of Bovine, Spongiform Encephalopathy (BSE) and its effects on beef prices as well as on the export hopes which had been so carefully built up for the Welsh Blacks. BSE was a disease which seemed to have sprung from nowhere; even now there is uncertainty about its origins. It is pitiful to see in affected animals; they cannot stand upright without difficulty and suffer an appalling death. It seems not to have affected all breeds equally; it made fewer inroads into Welsh Blacks than the average and there were a great many herds, my own included, where there was never a single case. I can assure my readers, that it was torment to walk the pastures in the morning, wondering what one was going to find. Every cattle-man dreaded discovering that his animals had come to the end of their BSE-Free status. I was lucky, but I can well imagine the dismay of those who found this disease in their herds.

A whole raft of new regulations followed, the most drastic was the preclusion from marketing as prime beef of animals aged over 30 months. It was assumed that the disease had its origin in the feeding of meat-and-bone meal, some of it insufficiently exposed to prescribed heat-levels in processing. There could be some foundation for this. The incidence peaked in 1992, when it was running at 500 cases per week across the UK, and abated when regulatory steps took effect. There are still very occasional cases today but, for practical purposes, we may feel optimistic that the end has been reached.

To begin with there were emphatic claims by the Government that BSE was entirely host-specific and would never cross over to humans. It did, in very small numbers only, but sufficient to cause terrible suffering where it did strike. Needless to say, it was also enough to stop a great many people eating beef. A new regulation, forbidding the consumption of beef on the bone, did nothing to help. Outside the UK, a ban was imposed everywhere on our beef exports as well as our exports of live breeding animals. Additionally, there were suggestions that this disease had an affinity with scrapie, which had been endemic in some sheep breeds for centuries.

Prices for beef fell, so did those of pedigree Welsh Blacks, except at the very top of the breed's class, which was the category my herd had reached at this time. The National Cattle Breeders' Association were, wisely, looking to the future of our standing as exporters of breeding stock. They urged all Societies to take a long view and to make certain they came out of this crisis with stock that had a very high health status and with a supply of semen and embryos of high quality and with reliable performance information. Welsh Blacks already had an excellent health status and very good traceability. We had a little semen, some of it from recorded animals, but not enough to stimulate the kind of turnover we needed to augment our limited internal trade. More ominously from our standpoint was the fact that Old Commonwealth countries were beginning to buy Welsh Black genetic material from each other.

Before I conclude the story of the foundation period of my herd, I should go back to the beginning and refer to some aspects of the breeding of Welsh Blacks which have been mentioned and which interested me profoundly, but which I was not able to take up.

The first of these is polling. I had never been one of those who said that you could assess the quality of an animal's bone by looking at its horns and gave this as reason enough to keep them. Neither would I propose that their roots in antiquity ought not to be disturbed. Although

polling had plenty of antagonists, its advocates were few and its practitioners even fewer. Therefore, the rules for up-grading to polled status were tough; there was no premium in the sale ring, and the protracted, half-way stages put stock at a distinct disadvantage. One of the breeders who succeeded with polling, in commercial as well as in breeding terms, was Mr. Dobie in Berwickshire. With 200 females, divided into two sub-herds, he had the kind of scope which others could only dream of.

There were some excellent breeders who made polling their cherished objective; at least half a dozen were really gifted men, yet they gave up, one by one. The last such was Lord Hooson. Shortly before his dispersal sale, he contributed a brilliant article to our journal, in which he described ways in which the Society might facilitate a gradual polling process by putting part-polled stock on an equal footing with horned animals; or else take on board a new scientific process involving the mating of animals with the correct mix of DNA-related factors.

That was a few years ago and, so far, nothing has come of it. Our pool of proven polled bulls is small, so the constraints on individuals are still formidable, and cattle are mostly de-horned, although the one Rare Breed, the Longhorn, is making a comeback. The immediate beneficiaries of an ability to offer polled stock would be owners of the leading herds of greatest interest to the commercial firms generating genetic material, for outlets where cattle are ranched and later put into feed-lots. The more polled cattle we can use, anyway, the better it would be for everyone, considering the time taken to achieve such an objective.

It comes back to the fact that exports are of benefit to everyone, not just the breeders directly engaged. Their success is necessary to every Welsh Black man who ever offers an animal for sale. An example of this is provided by Dai Davies, in his overview of his 21 years, beginning with an upsurge in prices arising from purchases by visiting Canadians. This faded away but, while it lasted, it had the effect of bucking the UK trend towards an awful collapse in prices. Some years later, when we were exporting 200 cattle to Germany each year, our prices did better than anyone could have imagined.

From this perspective, the introduction of a polling programme, using either of the methods advocated by Hooson, or even both, may be seen as a vital move. It would be unpopular and would remain so unless the membership generally could be persuaded that benefit would accrue to all pedigree breeders, and not just the few who are directly involved in the export trade. It would involve a determined initiative by Council, requiring courage as well as conviction. So far, I think the idea has had no serious consideration.

Next, I come to a side-issue of a rather personal nature, a minor, but by no means trivial preoccupation with the subject of coloured cattle. Our own Society will not register these, and

perhaps justifiably. I have had some coloured calves, duns, which were of remarkable quality. I castrated them all, of course, but with infinite regret. There are other coloured Welsh Blacks: red ones, in particular. Indeed, there is even a story to the effect that all Welsh cattle were originally red, and even that the dragon on our Welsh flag was, to begin with, a bull. That may be a bit fanciful, but there are some very good reds in Canada, where they are by no means kept concealed but are eligible for full registration. That may, or may not, be a good idea, but it does give me a twinge of heartache for my own beautiful duns. It is a pity they cannot be registered. The Australians would love to have them.

Something which I have been able to continue, although it is not connected with cattle, is my enthusiasm for Blue Merle sheep-dogs, an interest which I shared with our late Society Secretary, Gwilym Edwards. My father was the first person in our family to own one, and I can see why he valued them so much. Gwilym Edwards tried to get a Society going for these exceptional dogs, but he died before we could proceed. They have now been accepted into the Welsh Sheep Dog Society, despite the fact that they remain a minority preference. I am not looking for tremendous speed or staying power, let alone trials dogs, or those reputed to go in with that last bit of aggressive zeal. I need dogs with a subtle understanding of the nature of folded sheep, to do what is needed without causing upset. I also appreciate a loyal companion. I have had blue dogs all my life and their future at Brysgaga is assured.

I was unable to fit in performance recording with my immediate priority, which was to make my herd, still a very new one by Welsh Black standards, into a name which would be remembered from show-ring to sale ring, where it would attract the sort of prices which compared with those at the very top of the pyramid. None of this comes cheap. The cost of labour apart, show condition is not store condition, neither is the diet for show animals the same as for stores. The results must justify the investment, and, in my case, they did.

It might seem as if I had some premonition of the hard times to come, but I had none. I watched the prices made for recorded bulls fall until they were equal with the prices paid for any ordinary bulls. Then, in 1995, John Beynon, then President, announced that he had given up recording his Tyddewi herd after doing so for a considerable number of years. He felt that he was no longer justified in remaining in the pedigree market for he had never made an extra premium, however small, with a recorded bull. Nevertheless, he continued recording. It was a time when, in the domestic market, pedigree animals were considered something of an anomaly and yet our competitors were hard at it, offering genetic material for export as well as the domestic trade, complete with verifiable performance data. There were some excellent articles which Brinley Davies contributed to our journal, which I read with interest.

I had continued to hold to my ideas of co-operative working but now my mind began to follow a different tack. For the time being, such ideas had no practical application and I was not to know, then, that their time would come. There was no point, as John Beynon had said, in ploughing a lonely furrow but there could surely be some sort of co-operation. Not only would this have the advantage of cheapness, it would be a way of MAKING a flow, rather than having to follow an existing one. That was the path to exports and what they could do for the breed; it was not merely a way of letting the top breeders have an extra bite at the cherry. In my appraisal, in the cool light of day, this idea was no more than wild conjecture.

★★★★

After Dorothy and I moved into our bungalow at Comins Coch, we could see Brysgaga from the window. Unexpectedly, the beneficiary of our move away from the old farmhouse is Dorothy. Brysgaga is a beautiful house but to look after it with the love and care which she gave it is sheer slavery. That amount of hard work is unnecessary, if the home is no longer occupied by a family.

Dorothy laughed her way all round our bungalow. Housework now was the sort she could knock off in half an hour. People began to comment on the change in her as she blossomed. Men are selfish brutes, and I was not sorry that she had so much more time for me; she would soon need it, too, but that was in the future. Nonetheless, Brysgaga had been a life's work for her, she had undertaken it with so much imagination and had herself grown in expertise. We moved to a very ordinary bungalow but it did not stay that way for long. She found ways of accommodating many of her beautiful pieces without letting our home seem over-furnished, and made the whole atmosphere her own, in her very individual way. I found it strange, to begin with, to go home and leave the farm behind. I never really did that but, in many ways, I started living a more regulated life, and perhaps that is no bad thing.

Whether all this made Rowland feel more truly independent, I cannot tell. In business terms, much began to happen, not all of it welcome. As if BSE and all the associated regulations were not enough, we now saw the introduction of livestock quotas, and some land was subject to a new concept altogether: set-aside. There was a growing perception that farming would never be the same again; indeed, that it was only a matter of time before the smaller businesses went under. There was another new concept, too, and that was diversification.

Janice continued working after her marriage to Rowland, which could well have been her intention all along. She teaches Music at Aberaeron School and has an established career.

What she might not have done, in more favourable circumstances, was to continue without a break after the birth of their two children. Juggling job and family life can not be easy.

Rowland started to consider diversification and had two useful ideas. The first was the sale to retail customers of home-killed, well-hung beef, and the second was turf-laying. Amongst all the many schemes floated, we are already members of the Farm Assured Scheme, which embraces standards of husbandry as well as traceabilty for beef and sheep meat. Retailing beef seemed to offer an additional outlet, which was true, but only up to a point. Domestic customers have such a strong orientation towards personal convenience, that the idea of waiting until a beast has been killed and duly hung before being butchered was only attractive to a small number of people. Not only that, but it was an idea which occupied the minds of a good many others too, some of whom wanted to go it alone, while others sought various kinds of partnerships. It threatened to become an over-crowded free-for-all, with every man for himself. A venture based in Pembrokeshire, selling Welsh Black beef, has met with considerable difficulty, and it may be as well that Rowland had decided, for the time being, to keep this sideline within quite narrow limits.

His turf-laying business took off, is still growing and appears to have a bright future. The grass regeneration needed to make it profitable is as fast at Brysgaga as it was when my uncle cut turf on the tidal plain. In my bleaker, less tolerant moments, I reflect that a sideline, however profitable in its own right, can become too time-consuming, considering that it would never be crucial to the overall profitability of an enterprise the size of Brysgaga and the scale of its associated overheads, which must include, as it does today, the employment of outside help on the farm.

This brings me back to my uncle Dick and his heritage. I have never forgotten the time when, walking behind his hearse at his funeral, I hoped so fervently that I would find the strength to be worthy of him; not just to be a first-class breeder, but to be a man who could cope with adverse conditions with the same resolution and dignity as he had. What was not in my mind at that time was that what I might have to contend with would be very different from the troubles which threatened him. Then, we were entering a period of ever-increasing financial support for our industry, whatever the difficulties associated with guaranteed, fixed prices for our product. No one imagined that the cattle-farming business would be stood on its head after one generation. What faced my son, was exactly that.

It was a situation shared by the established farming families in our neighbourhood. Those with very small farms had no scope for alternatives. Their sons had, for some time, sought to supplement the family income by working outside. The owners of larger farms continued much as before, but they were not blind to what was happening. A few sold horticultural produce to private customers; others opted for Bed-and-Breakfast as a sideline; although I doubt whether this was ever really profitable, considering the very short holiday season we have in Wales. Most of them faced the future with misgiving. It was assumed that something must be done for agriculture, and that it would be done.

In view of all the changes in the industry, it may seem surprising that the first half of the nineteen-nineties saw the Welsh Black Society continue much as before. Our breed's excellent traceability and health status were distinct advantages in terms of BSE regulations. Additionally, there was a boost to prices, as people bought stock to realise their quota entitlements. Membership had slowly come down to half what it was in the Society's heyday, but this was less important than it might appear. There was no precipitate exodus but there had been the dispersal of large and famous herds belonging to landowners who were caught up in the Lloyds Members débâcle. The stock was still around, of course, but the loss of these excellent units would be no help to our future.

In the immediate term, it was a matter of urgency that we should be able to maintain our prices. Up to a point, we did. BSE began to wane. The Society had to make ends meet. Dai Davies, our Secretary, now nearing the end of his tenure, reflected the attitudes and views of Council as he always had. No one could foresee that, within a year of taking office, our new Secretary, Evelyn Jones, would announce, 'Opportunity knocks!'

CHAPTER TWELVE
The Scourge of Foot and Mouth Disease

At the end of the last chapter I quoted from the first annual report by our new Society Secretary, Evelyn Jones: 'Opportunity knocks,' she said. She referred to our success in gaining a European grant under the 5b Scheme for poorer areas in the Union. This was to cover three years initially, followed subsequently by a similar grant covering two further years. The amount was made up mainly by a direct grant, plus a contribution from the Welsh Assembly and another from the Welsh Black Society itself, which held as existing assets in reserve the total sum of three quarters of a million pounds.

The first step was the appointment of a 5b Development Officer, Mr. Andrew James. The remit was, broadly, to foster the development and improvement of the only native cattle breed in Wales, and was summarised under the following categories:

Education and training for younger breeders - Travelling scholarships;
specialised courses,

e.g. carcass evaluation;
artificial insemination;
grassland usage.

Further development of herd-based animal health schemes,
aiming at the widest possible participation of all breeders.

Group-based use of MLC's herd-improvement procedures,
to generate objective performance data for the enhancement of
profitability-potential across Welsh Black herds.

Collection and marketing of genetic material i.e. semen and fertilised embryos from top-quality sires and dams,to stimulate trade as well as breed-improvement.

Initially, we were unable to count on the two-year extension I have mentioned, and even a five-year period is short when one considers the long-term nature of the main components of the scheme. There was no time to be lost if we were to gain maximum benefit.

There has been no difficulty in co-ordinating the various health schemes because our health status has always been very good but we are also helped by the high degree of traceability we have enjoyed for some long time. We have been able to attack Johne's disease in a very convincing manner and seen the last, I hope, of the really serious scourges. We have wonderful support from the retired Welsh Veterinary Officer, Bruce Lawson. The great benefit of all this is that it has encouraged stock farmers to see animal health on a herd basis rather than looking to the treatment of individual animals. E. L.'s forecast about the status of animal heath came back to my mind.

It is not hard to select suitable young Welsh Black breeders for travelling scholarships, or to find enthusiastic participants for the very useful short courses which were set up with the willing co-operation of many specialised establishments, including Pwllpeiran with its great upland-grazing expertise. It was more difficult to secure the active co-operation of breeders in the envisaged breed-improvement projects, which were the core of the whole thing.

As time went on, each of its two parts would complement the other. If such a concept was to be considered seriously it would make a huge impact on present practice. We were now asking breeders to participate in something which had never enjoyed active support and which, in the eyes of many, had been the object of downright derision. What was planned would go a lot further than anything that had been proposed previously. The introduction of sire-referencing by the BLUP scheme built on the same principle, but it had the object of facilitating comparisons between animals of the same breeds, in different herds. Briefly, this meant putting the same 'reference sire' over a proportion of each of a number of different units and comparing the progeny of the reference sire against those of others, both internally and right across the board.

A bull which has become famous for show successes, or even just on the strength of his prefix, is worth a lot of money. If his bloodline were disseminated widely by the sale of semen, or if his BLUP index turned out to be indifferent, this would adversely affect his worth. There were commitments attaching to this new system the consequences of which were uncertain.

I recall that there was little discussion on the subject. People were assessing the projects from a personal point of view, and so was I. My opinion was that this was exactly what was wanted. Brinley Davies had not left me unimpressed; rather, I had only been deterred by the thought of going ahead on my own. Now, the old co-operator stirred in me and my big ideas suddenly seemed less eccentric after all.

By a quirk of fate, it fell to me to be our Society's President Elect in 1997-8, and President in the following year. I am far from being a fatalist, but I cannot deny that, as Shakespeare put it,

1998, Dilwyn Jenkins (son of W. B. breeder Bennet Jenkins), and his daughter Caryl in the new lounge at the Royal Welsh Showground

'There is a tide in the affairs of man ....'.

To start with, I wrote a provocative appeal in the Society's *Journal*, 'Are you part of the game?' I demanded. I urged members to participate in the health scheme and in the selection process for animals which might yield suitable genetic material. I also extolled the virtue of the BLUP principle, insisting that it was a necessary path to genuine competition with other breeds as well as the improvement of our own. I followed this up, in the customary overview of the new president's *curriculum vitae*, with further urging on the same lines.

It is usual for a President to make some sort of gift to the coffers of the Society. I gave £1,500 and specified that it was be used towards the cost of adding an extension to our new O. G. Thomas building at the Royal Welsh show ground, to accommodate a special Marketing Lounge. Marketing is just what it says. I believed that there was more to it than the marketing of Welsh Black cattle. Beef was not included in the 5b Scheme, and if I had anything to do with it, that would come. Now, it was time for me to start work.

Gwyn Howells at MLC co-ordinated the BLUP Scheme and put in a lot of hard work. He co-operated with us in amending the scheme to accommodate items which were special to Welsh Blacks, such as maternal qualities; although these could stand some more revision, such things can follow as we go along. However, he was very short of backup staff, and the new parent body, Signet, at Milton Keynes, had, and still has, difficulty getting its administration bedded down sufficiently to obviate elementary clerical errors, many of which could have quite serious consequences.

Nevertheless, there are now 40 members in the BLUP Scheme, i.e. ten per cent of active breeders of Welsh Blacks, recording well over 1,000 animals annually. By any standards and by the measure of other breeds that is an excellent achievement. It meant we had the scope to get real improvement over the generations, not just for exports, but to penetrate the national herd by offering high-performance bulls at sales. Given some further funding, in part if not in total, to help us to carry on beyond the term of 5b, the future in this respect is assured.

I did my best to find converts to the scheme, which has two main arguments in its favour. One is the benefit to the national herd from a truly co-operative effort by the best breeders, if the overall characteristics and profitability-potential of the breed can go forward by the use of these two schemes. The other is a plea for a long-term stance in respect of individual herds. While it is true, especially at the outset, that occasionally a famous bull might lose market-value through the proliferation of his genes, a mine of information opens up on the characteristics of bloodlines within a herd which must, as time goes on, become indispensable to anyone who does not turn a blind eye to the future.

The future development of the breed, admittedly, needs some audacity of approach and it is not easy to be persuaded of this if you are already enjoying the proven fruits of great success. In response to my initial call in the *Journal* there was silence.

Given the support we have from a wide spectrum of very good breeders, and younger ones especially, there is reason for optimism if we can keep going long enough to show some demonstrable results. Some good has come out of it already. A quantity of semen and embryos sold well to starter-herds. The benefit of this is not so easy to quantify but we have now reached a stage where we are finding it less easy to provide enough supplies of semen and embryos to meet demand.

Even without funding, this side of the enterprise should not be too difficult to keep going, because of the involvement of the commercial firms which recover and trade in the material. Without the backup of objective data this aspect of marketing would be less useful, but at least it gives us one foot in the door. I put forward a couple of animals for the collection of genetic material and made my way up the ladder in the BLUP Scheme. My success was probably due to the fact that I had run a closed herd for so long, the bulls I had bought in were few in number and their breeding was thoroughly researched. I knew exactly what I could expect from most matings.

With everyone starting at zero, late-starters, or less well established herds, could be at a disadvantage. This possibility was recognised and addressed by the recent awards for the herds

achieving the steepest improvement-curve. Certainly, it introduces an extra dimension into breeding policy and, since the profit-criterion is the nub of the indexing system, this is surely what cattle-breeding is all about.

Andrew James did a really good job in arranging for the presentation of animals for assessment for collection of genetic material. We had a large number of offers, perhaps partly in response to the fee to breeders which this involved. It was clear that the stock on offer needed to be looked over on the home farms, so that the related animals could be seen as well.

We established a number of small teams of breeders and made seemingly endless visits. This was of consuming interest for me, if only for the sake of the insight it offered into herds which might be quite obscure and whose progeny had only been seen in small numbers when they were presented at sales. There were some with genuine potential. It can be surprising what you find, and where. We found one very good bull at the kite-conservation centre, which is open to the public, and where this poor beauty was condemned to being ogled at for a small fee.

So far, we have staged two assessment occasions, one in 1998 for older bulls; and a more elaborate one, for younger bulls, in 2002, held at a public gathering at the Royal Welsh show ground and featuring a grand parade of the 40 excellent animals presented. That second gathering furnished us with the right kind of publicity. There was real quality in the stock paraded. The points system, to cover various features individually, was based on the following criteria: Signet Beef Value, where applicable; breed characteristics; general conformation and presentation; bloodline-background. The public were free to observe the panels at work. They had not come to be entertained, there was genuine interest.

There was hope in the air. Old men have always complained that farming would never be the same again. We could, I was sure, continue to improve our animals. Those lean carcasses with excellent conformation and size, to say nothing of the superb marbling of the meat, had a sales advantage crying out to be placed before our environment-conscious consumers. The animals were finished on grass, good, natural stuff. What I felt was needed, was not the *ad hoc* supplying to occasional customers by farmers marketing their beef as and when available, but the systematic targeting of niche markets by a Welsh Black Beef Marketing Group engaged in procurement and selling.

I aired the idea in Council and was appointed chairman of a steering committee to serve this purpose. Initially, we had to attract funding, and this would only be made available to us if we came up with the suitable match-funding which was always required for such applications. I sent out an appeal to breeders, asking them to contribute £12 each. The response was sufficiently promising to enable us to put a scheme together for submission to the Welsh Development Agency, in the form of a Strategy Report.

Highlight of my presidential year was the time spent at the bi-centenary Smithfield Show, in 1998, at which our native Welsh Blacks did so well. Mr Goronwy Jones's steer came reserve for the Queen's Cup, and the team of 3 were reserve in the overall inter-breed group competition for The Duke of Norfolk Cup. There was a great atmosphere when the decision was announced, and the Welsh contingent applauded and made their presence felt. The atmosphere was reminiscent of that other great Welsh occasion, when Scott Gibbs scored his memorable try, followed by Neil Jenkins's conversion, to defeat England at Wembley, in the same year. A tingle went down one's spine.

Winning at home, or even at Stoneleigh, was one thing; London, with all that noisy support from our own compatriots, was another thing altogether. If I had to pinpoint one memorable event in my presidency that would be the one I would choose.

Another show which filled me with pride was one held by the German breeders of Welsh Blacks, early in 1999. The Germans don't hold shows in the way we do, but the Welsh Black breeders had attended the Royal Welsh and had been to Smithfield, so now they put on a show of their own. They invited us and did us proud as their guests. They had 55 good entries. It was clear that the husbandry was good and, as breeders, our friends knew what they were about. Above all, our cattle were appreciated and had adapted well and here was further proof of their versatility. It was a shame that we were still under BSE restrictions but we thought we could hope for better times, when our joint efforts would find their reward.

I also counted it a privilege to have been present at the AGM, show and reception put on by the English Section of our Society, at the home of the Dimory Seeks, in Somerset. There was a judging competition, too. Many of the participants were new to Welsh Blacks, so it was especially important in this context. This section is still spread thinly over the whole of England, so their difficulties are considerable. It is thanks to a few individuals that it has been held together over so many years. The south-western part of England is now included in our South Wales herd competition. We have given them support over time; I only wish we could do more.

I attended the Royal Highland at Ingliston, in Scotland, where we Welsh have been taught to feel at home in a special Scottish way. We certainly appreciate the quality of the Scottish Welsh Blacks. There was the Royal at Stoneleigh and our own Royal Welsh, but I also wanted to visit as many of the smaller shows as I possibly could. These include Aberystwyth, where I arranged with Dewi Roberts of Llandeilo, an expert in this field, to sell beef from one of my registered Welsh Black steers in the President's marquee; Talsarn; Talybont; the Anglesey Show; and the Nefyn Show. I was judge at Cothi Bridge and the shows at Anglesey and at Pembroke.

Lord Hooson, a foremost pioneer of polled cattle, held an open day and a dispersal sale a short time later. I was present at both, with some regret. The cattle were excellent and it seemed a pity they would no longer go forward as a unit. I also attended our Society sales at Ruthin and Llandovery, and all our sales at Dolgellau. This is recognised as our major venue, and I was able to meet the auctioneers to explore ways of improving these sales further.

There were odd jobs to be done, too: such as collecting our Welsh Black decorative plates from the potter at Tywyn; interviewing two candidates for travelling scholarships under the 5b Scheme, both of them good, and attending a RABI meeting (Royal Agricultural Benevolent Institution) on behalf of WBCS. A radio interview, I suppose, also comes into this bracket.

Then I discovered we were behind with painting the new Marketing Lounge in readiness for its formal opening at the forthcoming Royal Welsh Show. So I got busy. I was painting busily when a photographer turned up and, sure enough, I ended up in the press, pictured as the Painting President. If that was the only way to get the painting done, so be it. The opening proved an impressive occasion.

Impressive in another way was the 90th birthday party for Bety Davis, at Llanina. She is not just a foremost breeder and well-known local personality, she has been one of our more famous Presidents, and is still active and wise as a Life-President. Such functions are an essential part of a president's year of office. Most members might attend a few of them; to cover the whole lot can be quite a tall order, but I found them more worthwhile than I had anticipated.

Early on, we had a huge beef roast at Caernarfon in aid of WBCS. That was when I realised how generous our members are. We were, after all, not yet out of the wood after BSE and all the damage that did to our trade and our prices. At the Beef Roast we collected a total of £4,700 in aid of WBCS. This was an excellent beginning towards a total over the whole year of £11,000, from an overall membership of 800.

Another function I must mention here is one which cost me no small embarrassment. That was the occasion of the *beef-on-the-bone* episode, at the reception given for the launch of Welsh Beef & Lamb Promotions Ltd. At that time it was still illegal to sell beef attached to a part of the spine, such as T-Bone steaks, for example. We knew this restriction was soon to end and nobody cared about it, anyway, so we had it on our buffet menu. However, it's different when you offer such a steak to the Prince of Wales and he is photographed, tucking in heartily to forbidden goodies. Oh yes, I was beside him, also enjoying the feast.

Dorothy was my tireless companion at all these functions, and I was to try her patience even further, for she was with me throughout my travels when I did the inspections for the South Wales herd competition. At our many destinations, we were received with so much kindness that this, alone, would have made our journeys memorable. There was amusement, too. Once, I locked myself into my car and had to be retrieved by my host, Aneurin Francis, who used his ingenuity to extricate me with a wire as his sole tool to unlock the door. The fun went rather far, on the same visit, when I was taken on a 4X4 bike ride up the steep slopes of Pistyll Uchaf, which were the nearest to a Wall of Death that I have ever come!

Adventures and practical geography apart, these visits taught me a lot. It was in settings like this that one could appreciate that the breed has improved tremendously over the years. In the course of my inspections I looked for evidence, such as the presence of some superior animals, that the breeder was in the process of improving his stock, or that he had already gone a long way in this direction and had left a personal stamp on its character. I would want to know something about his approach to pedigrees: whether he concentrated on the superior animals they contained, or took due account of the poorer ones, whose influence can do so much damage.

I also assessed the quality of general nutrition and grassland management. Oddly, the judge of the previous competition had complained she had found ragwort everywhere. I suggested that, since cast ewes were so cheap and plentiful, a batch of these would soon eat it all up. I was keen to see whether precautions had been taken where heavy rainfall had left such an abundance of grass that there might be a danger of staggers. I wanted to see some straw put out, to steady the rumen action, and I always like licks to be made available, to ensure a good balance of minerals.

Finally, I looked for an up-to-date attitude to herd health, which goes beyond the general appearance of bloom. I found that this was very good, and was glad to see that our various health and certification schemes were taken seriously, and, as far as I could see, to good effect. It will be clear from all this that I spent a lot of time on each of these inspections, 18 of them in all. I enjoyed each one, and am grateful for all I learnt from them.

There were visits of a more routine character, such as one I paid to a breeder who had stopped registering his Welsh Blacks but wanted to start again. There is a standard procedure for such applications, to ensure that the animals concerned are satisfactory. I used all the criteria I applied to the competition judging.

The year of my presidency saw the arrival at Brysgaga of Dafydd. I had followed my father; bought the farm; seen Rowland follow me; and now there was Dafydd. Now, we were J.P., D.M. & R.A. Rees & Son – members of FAWL & Signet Elite Club, with a herd which was EBL attested, BSE free.

Although I had retired, as much as any farmer is ever fully retired, and was living in a village housing development, I was never absent from the farm on any permanent basis. Most other Society Presidents have been working farmers, too. Somehow, we have all found ways to manage our time, to fit in everything we wanted to accomplish. It meant attending all the major events: Smithfield, the English Show and AGM in the West Country, the Royal at Stoneleigh, the Royal Welsh, and all the other big ones. I have no time to mention all the little ones I also visited.

There are meetings, large and small, and functions where one goes not just to see and to be seen, but for the opportunity to hobnob with those at the grass roots and the great and the good. There is always something to be mentioned to somebody, someone to be coaxed into acceptance of an aspect of policy, and other times, when it falls to me to make sure people feel appreciated, and all the while one practises the art of nursing a glass without actually drinking.

The President's position within the Council of the Society is not defined in great detail, beyond the expectation that he will contribute wherever he can. To the extent that there is already a sitting chairman, not only for the Council itself, but for every sub-committee as well, and it is obvious, in any case, that no one can be everywhere all the time, there is some good sense in leaving this aspect a little vague. Nonetheless, I did manage maximum attendance.

Our 5b Chairman and committee did their job very well, but the President was a sort of roving emissary, whose job was to instil enthusiasm where the decisive influence would reside in any future dispensations. Sometimes I intervened where there was less conviction amongst breeders who were not well known, than there was amongst breeders who were producing quality and were already famous; largely, these were officials of the Society. There could be an element of short-term self-interest amongst these better known breeders, in addition to their attachment to tradition, with the dangerous corollary that they sometimes felt that there is nothing left to learn. In tackling them, I was taking on The Establishment.

I had the right qualifications for the job. I was a regular exhibitor on the show-circuit, had won substantial prizes and had done my share of judging; and my sale-prices matched the show successes. No one could suggest I had not exercised the traditional skills and instincts, and used my eye, so my advocacy of the use of number-crunching as a tool, not as a substitute for these time-honoured skills, could be seen as entirely credible. Similarly true was my insistence that the market owes us nothing; we have to give it what it wants if we are to stimulate exports as well as UK interest, and so raise our own sale-ring prices.

If one works on the assumption that repetition, not a sudden blast of trumpets, is the way to make a message sink in, then you must be persuasive rather than forceful, and this, as it happened, suited me very nicely. Not only that: we are all Welshmen. No one was ever aggressive.

I hope and believe that I did leave some footprints in the sand; whether they were deep enough to withstand any storms which might blow over them only time can tell.

There was a lot to look back on with a smile, and many interesting characters to remember. One of the highlights of the Millennium First RWAS, apart from the Grand Slam achieved by the Welsh

Black Cattle breed, was the Pageant Exhibition organised and exhibited by the Welsh Black Society. Forming part of the exhibition were the Welsh Black oxen, pulling a fully loaded sledge and in the charge of Mr William Jones, Caerberllan, his brother and helpers. When I spoke to him afterwards, he recalled how he used to ride on the back of a calf, to cross the river to collect the cows for hand milking and suckling, and bring them into the cow shed. On one occasion, he was unlucky enough to be caught on his side by a gate hinge, and he recalled how the doctor tending him remarked that he was too young a chicken to be 'stitched up'.

Another occurrence, that took place some years ago, happened to one of the most dedicated stockmen of our time. After attending to his stock late at night, he was travelling home in his van. Being an elderly gentleman, nearing his pension, he always drove slowly and very carefully, but because he was out at that time of night, he was stopped by an over eager young policeman. Having stopped the vehicle, the PC poked his nose through the window for a real good sniff, and the Blue Merle sheep dog, that was sitting quietly in the passenger seat, nearly bit his nose off.

Then, there was a certain Welsh Black breeder, and quite a character, who met another breeder, a woman who, unknown to him, had remarried.

'Duw, how are you, Mrs Jones fach?' he greeted her.

To which she replied, 'I'm Mrs Williams now.'

'Duw, Duw, Mrs Jones fach, you'll always be

Mrs Jones to us,' he said.

There is a tale told of Professor Williams, chair of WAOS, who was at the bar and asked a friend what he would like to drink.

His friend replied, 'I'll have a whisky, please.'

'Good,' said the Professor, 'and I'll have a double.'

Another tale that went around concerned the Welsh language. Apparently, at a recent sitting of the magistrates' court in Dolgellau, the presiding magistrate asked the defendants which language they would prefer the court to use when putting forward a defence in their case. Mr Williams indicated English; Mr Jones also said English; Mr Davies, too, elected to have English; and Mr Roberts wanted English; but the Polish man unhesitatingly replied *Cymraeg*.

★★★★

Immediately after retirement, you contemplate this eternity that stretches ahead of you, and wonder how you will ever get through it, but you get used to it. Another thing I was to get used to, and infinitely more satisfying than anything else, was the arrival of another generation at Brysgaga, in the small person of Dafydd. I had followed my father; bought the farm; seen Rowland follow me; and now there was Dafydd! The sense of elation is hard to convey, quite apart from the joy which every baby brings into every family.

Janice went back to work, but she managed wonderfully. Somehow, Dafydd seemed to give her more hours in the day; she had time for him, for Rowland, for everything; even for her splendid garden. Who said hers was a lousy, selfish generation?

As children, Janice and Rowland had grown up with a very different view of the business side of agriculture from the one which confronted them now. In the nineteen-sixties and early nineteen-seventies, everything turned on efficient productivity. There was also the fact that guide prices changed with the seasons, and only marginally with supply, to say nothing of demand or quality. There were subsidies for every farm-improvement measure you could think of, except for investments in better livestock. They covered everything else, from liming to fencing and more. The newspapers were angled towards urban readers, and complained that farmers were feather-bedded.

The time came when there was, indeed, serious over-production in agriculture across Europe and elsewhere. To deal with it, the CAP (Common Agricultural Policy) was introduced, when we joined the Common Market. Now, we had Intervention prices, which gave a secure outlet for produce and led, inevitably, to the growth of butter-mountains, beef-mountains, wine-lakes and the rest. The outcome was seen as a scandal, and in some ways it was just that, but the CAP was apparently immovable. There have been gripes about Brussels and justified complaints about the high levels of the so-called Green Pound as a conversion figure, but one would have to say it was the best lifeline we ever had, and it meant that small farms, which would not be viable today, still yielded a decent living and contributed a great deal to the stability of the rural community, especially in Wales.

Inevitably, CAP had disadvantages, too. It did little to encourage enterprise, let alone the improvement of stock offered for sale at a commercial level. It led to the creation of a false sense of security and bred a culture of dependency. It was to be seen especially on the smaller farms. The consequence brought disappointment, later on. When major changes did arrive, only the more businesslike farmers saw the opportunities. The price-regime was scrapped at a stroke. Instead, we saw the introduction of headage payments, on a quota system based on previous stocking-rates.

Trading became more sophisticated. Much depended, now, on a strategic choice of markets. At the bottom end, there was probably far too much movement of stock, eating up overheads and, ultimately, causing calamity. The rewards for quality were beginning to show. If the stock was good, there was interest from abattoirs looking for suitable product at better prices. If you were also Farm Assured, that was an added advantage. The concept of a market economy was gaining ground.

Younger farmers began to use computers, not only for management purposes, but to benefit from the Internet as well. The gap between the enterprising and the rest was beginning to widen, not just in prices realised, but in costs of production as well. It was inevitable that some

people would be left behind, not only owners of the smaller businesses, but, to a large extent, those who were already over-borrowed.

The BSE-crisis, with all its attendant anxieties and a host of regulations, had made it difficult to take full advantage of the new provisions. A worse aspect to this was the loss of our export markets for beef and sheep meat, which did a great deal of damage to the finances of most stock-farms. For a farm like Brysgaga, which had always prospered, and which had stock well able to compete in the commercial market, there could be reason for optimism. Nevertheless, there was a steep mountain to climb.

That was when Dafydd, followed by Daniel, was born. After her confinements, Janice went back to work, and everybody was always cheerful.

★★★★

Most presidents hold open days on their farms, in order to give members a jolly good day out. We are all human and we do our best to show off our stock as well, so it is not like preparing a show-team; the whole lot, sheep as well, must put their best feet forward, and you are hard at it for some months before the event.

The great day itself is an exercise in logistics. You assemble a whole fleet of tractors and trailers, with seating as comfortable as you can make it, and old age and decrepitude are no bar to outings of this kind. You place your stock in strategic areas, where they can be seen at reasonably close quarters. In our case, that meant organising this kind of show at Brysgaga, with all the trappings and transport. You pray for good weather. We were a little unlucky, for the weather on that day was indifferent.

Finally, something must be done to help your visitors keep body and soul together. Most people engage an outside caterer, but we went one better. Rowland had the bright idea that, if IGER could be given a little piece of the action, they would be happy to let us use their premises for a grand bash and a real feast, with a proper beef-roast, no less. He was right. IGER were as enthusiastic as we were. Never satisfied, Rowland went further. He wondered why our commercial suppliers should not be asked to contribute items for a grand auction, to raise money for the Society. He approached them all, and it is surprising how generous they were. This could have been, perhaps, because they had never been asked to help in this way before, and had no cause to groan, 'Oh, no, not another one!' They came up with all sorts of things, even a valuable hot/cold pressure-washer.

Andrew James went on to ask why the stewarding should not be done by the local Talybont Young Farmers' Club. When he asked them, they were delighted, and those too young for such jobs were invited anyway, as special guests.

The event had the purpose of showing off a mature and well-known herd to fellow-breeders, who were also to be entertained by their President; but with Rowland as the driving force behind it, the event had the freshness and energy of youth.

On the day itself, all this showed in the atmosphere. With 500 people to take around, a large number for an event of this kind, something extra was unmistakable. The old entered into the spirit of it no less than the young, and the whole thing went with a swing. It was remarkable, and so was the follow-up at IGER. Anyone would think that, after all this travelling about, the guests would be too exhausted to look at the show of experimental work put on for them. Not a bit of it! When it came to the grand finale, the big beef-roast, there was plenty of energy left to do it full justice. Lots of generosity from those who attended helped the auction in aid of the Society's funds to make £4,600.

None of this could have succeeded as it did without the contribution of the great things which characterised our Welsh Black occasions over such a long time: the humour and the sense of theatre. If I may wax sentimental here, I would add that the success also derived from our love of the land.

There was a difference, though, from other such presidential parties. This was a father-and-son show, in a modern sense. Perhaps something else showed, that I did not see myself as the traditional worthy breeder with the Presidency as the zenith of his career. This was an opportunity and a beginning of the future. The confidence of members was what I needed now, to pursue my hopes for the future of the breed as I saw it.

Such hopes were not without foundation. Attitudes change. Above all, BSE and its attendant complications were fading and, by the end of the year 2000, we believed we could safely look forward to an early resumption of our export trade.

Now, too, it would be easier to get the aim across to members and convince them to regard the export of high-performance stock and/or its genetic material as a means of lifting our domestic prices in the sale-ring, with improved stock on offer, once our programme had got under way.

I was sure, too, that a successful organisation to back up our beef-trade could provide, in addition to direct benefits to producers, sales figures showing enhanced prices obtainable for our beef. This, surely, would not be lost, either on customers abroad, or on members in UK, of whom some would be direct beneficiaries of premium prices already.

To get started, we would need a marketing officer and some initial funding to cover the first three years or so. Our application and business plan were already in the hands of WDA. Any President wants to put his term of office to the best possible use. I was fortunate in arriving in post at a time of great opportunity. Evelyn Jones had been right.

I knew from the outset, that not all our 5b scheme components would meet with unqualified enthusiasm but, by the end of my term of office, I had reason to think that there was sufficient change in the general mindset to ensure that our

1965 – John Rees and Tom Raw-Rees protesting at low farm prices

innovations were here to stay. No one person can claim to have been the engineer of it all. I knew, however, that it was no bad thing to have a genuine enthusiast as the serving President at that crucial time.

I was soon to wonder whether '*the tide in the affairs of man,*' of which I had felt so conscious at the beginning of my term of office, would go crashing against an obstacle as large as it was unforeseeable, and bring all our efforts to naught.

Throughout this book, I have referred to the economic depression of the nineteen-thirties, and how, during my life-time, the wheel has turned almost full circle and brought the farming industry back into a severe slump. There have been several mini recessions in the years between. There was the Fair Deal Campaign, in 1965, when Mr. Tom Raw-Rees, Brynbŵl, and I demonstrated outside the Royal Pier Pavilion, when the then Minister of Agriculture, Ted Peart, was due to address the W. A. O. S. AGM. The man who was standing as the prospective Labour candidate for Cardiganshire, Mr. D. J. Davies of Pantyrod, hurled himself at Mr. Tom Raw-Rees and tried to grab his placard. Consequently, the press reporters and photographers had a field-day, and the story made the headlines in the following day's newspapers, although there was, consequently, little mention of the W.A.O.S. AGM.

Later on, we demonstrated against the auction of Irish cattle, and one of our slogans was,

'*Adre! Adre! Wartheg Afradlon!*' (Go home! Go home! Wasteful Cattle!) This also made the headlines in the farming press. In 1974, there was the Beef Crisis, when subsidised beef from abroad was being 'dumped' in the U. K. Farmers again put up a vehement protest and marched to the ports to try and stop the imported meat from being unloaded. There was a nasty incident at Holyhead, when cartons containing imported beef were thrown into the sea. I recall Vincent Kane, interviewing Tom Raw-Rees on the subject of Irish cattle auctions in Wales, when Tom fearlessly said that, in his opinion, the place for Irish cattle was at the bottom of the sea.

All these incidents, coming with regularity during the time I was growing up and forming my association with the Welsh Blacks, led to my involvement with the W. A. O. S. and the Federation of Agricultural Co-operatives; and, at a European level, when I was a representative on the G. O. G. E. C. A., the co-ordinating body for co-operation with the E. E. C. Farming, for me, was an eternal battle to see fair play and to gain advantage for our home-produced, high quality meat. There were some things, however, against which no amount of foresight and planning on our part was to prove effective.

Early in 2001, the unimaginable happened: foot-and-mouth disease was discovered amongst pigs in Yorkshire, and a nightmare began, during which it was hard to laugh at anything, because the situation was so serious and we were uncertain what its extent would be. Somebody remarked that our vets could not cope and that we would have to import vets from Europe to help. Somebody else then remarked that they already had a Spaniard in their practice, and it was very hard to understand what he was saying, especially when he had a hypodermic syringe in his mouth.

CHAPTER THIRTEEN
The Aftermath

Foot and Mouth Disease affected all our lives. No one knew where it would strike next, or when it would be brought under control. Having to see healthy stock slaughtered seemed an affront to us all. No wonder it had a disastrous effect on the mental health of some individuals.

The prospect of compensation was no comfort either, and, throughout the UK, stock-breeders were united in trying to overcome the infection. Rivalries, animosities, were forgotten. All you could do was examine your stock carefully, daily, and take every possible precaution. We lived, almost literally, in a state of siege.

I suppose we have to say that, in Ceredigion, we were lucky. We had no cases at all. Overall, Welsh Blacks lost 11 herds, but the impact of the restrictions, almost everywhere, was ruinous. There were herds, designated as contiguous to affected herds, which could not be moved in any circumstances, regardless even of welfare considerations. There were movement restrictions which were, later, subject to the herd owner first obtaining special licences, a cumbersome business.

In some circumstances, you could send animals for slaughter, although there were no markets held, or any other venues of any kind open to receive the animals.

This dire situation lasted for fully seven months. Even as I write, we cannot repeat any animal movement in less than twenty days from the last one. It is surprising that so few people gave up farming altogether. Certainly, it will take all of us a long time to recover from the damage Foot and Mouth Disease has done.

Much thought has been given to the causes of this terrible outbreak and the speed of its spread and, especially, to the tendency for commercial producers to specialise, and the consequent growth in the frequency of animal movements and the distances they travel. All sorts of suggestions for ensuring the disease does not reappear have been advanced. There should be more control of imports, and of so-called rotten apples, of whom, regrettably, there are bound to be a few in a farming population of many thousands. All this leads nowhere at all. Instead, we should avoid the idea that contemporary farming is the cause of it all and we would be better served by the kind of husbandry that went back to basics, in other words, organic farming. I cannot judge organic horticulture, or any speciality, except stock-breeding.

When my father took over Brysgaga, he started with a milking herd of ten. That was all that the farm would support, with a system of self-sufficiency, so far as nutrition was concerned, and with a limitation on the use of fertilisers as we know them today. He advanced to a herd of 35 cows because his methods of husbandry moved along with the times. Organic farming, by definition, would mean going back to this kind of husbandry, but it would have to be practised within an outside environment which is different from that inside the home farm. It remains to be seen whether, in the absence of the prophylactic use of antibiotics, these herds will remain immune from the common infections with which they are bound to come into contact.

Of more immediate importance is the impact of this method of organic farming on the financial side of such enterprises. To maintain any given number of cows would need far more land than is needed otherwise, and this represents more husbandry costs as well as a larger initial investment. To produce like-for-like, under such conditions, would require a premium in the market that is far higher than the consumer would bear.

My own concern is centred on the possible effects of more limited nutrition, and the damage this might do to the breed as a whole. What I have seen so far confirms my fears: there appears to be some loss of size, and it has happened very quickly. If we want to compete as a premier beef-breed, with first-class suckler-cows to match, I can't believe that this is the way to go.

The affairs of the Welsh Blacks, in a narrower sense, were at a standstill during this crisis. 5b was on hold, to all intents and purposes. We could still weigh our stock on-farm, if we were lucky, but there could be no such thing as selection for semen collection. Surprisingly, membership of the BLUP scheme went down by only six herds.

Perhaps there was a feeling that nothing would ever be the same again. Our Secretary, Evelyn Jones, left us. Andrew James, who had come to us as our 5b co-ordinator, is now our Chief Executive Officer. The WBCS Journal has been discontinued, because it was written mainly for members and was not sufficiently outward-looking. The final issue, Vol. 4, No. 6, was published in 2001, at which time the recorded membership of the WBCS stood at 851. It would have been sad to lose this publication, which was one way in which far flung members were able to retain contact with others. Although the journal was stopped at the time of Foot and Mouth, I am glad to say that it is to continue in future. We have not suffered a major exodus of members; even a fall-off in registrations has been small and by no means catastrophic. We are beginning to move about again. Even though our Royal Welsh entries in 2002 were less numerous than we might have hoped, it was still a brave show.

There is always something we can do. For instance, it was clear to the organisers of the Llanilar show that there was little hope of attracting cattle entries because of the twenty-day movement restriction. The only way to get over the difficulty was to have a herd competition and to celebrate the results at the show. It worked. Actually, it proved a very sensible innovation and something may well come of it later on, when we are no longer driven to invention by necessity.

Finding ways of overcoming difficulties is part of practical farming. I wish I could say the same of my experience of administrative agencies. I am not carping at what was done, or left undone, in the context of the Foot and Mouth crisis. We can all be clever with the benefit of hindsight, but it seemed to me that everything else to do with promoting our breed, whether connected with Foot and Mouth or not, was in limbo. I refer, of course, to plans for the marketing of beef.

Before I begin to relate this tale, here are the various agencies involved with agricultural matters:

The Welsh Development Agency;
The Food Directory of the above;
Welsh Food Promotions, and its offshoot
Welsh Lamb & Beef Promotions Ltd. (WLBP)
The Agriculture Dept. of the Welsh Assembly;
The Welsh Assembly.

In the background:
The Welsh Office.

To contend with all this, I chair our Society's Steering Committee, which oversees the formation of the Welsh Black Beef Marketing Group. This, as I have mentioned already, was set up in response to my representations to Council on the subject of niche-marketing our excellent end-product.

We held two meetings jointly with Council and the Steering Committee. What emerged was the plan that we should seek funding to set up a marketing agency, which would employ a full-time officer to ensure the targeting of markets, to obtain the best premium value for our product as well as the best publicity. We realised that we would have to provide match-funding on a pound-for-pound basis if such an application were to be entertained.

With a loan of £1,000 from WBCS and the £12 contributed by each of 130 members, I was able to lodge £2,500 at NatWest Bank. There was also an envisaged commitment of £9,000 from Welsh Black Beef Marketing Ltd.

On this basis, we submitted an application to the Food Directorate of the Welsh Development Agency, in March, 2000, for three-year start-up support for a Welsh Black Beef Procurement Agency with a full-time marketing officer plus clerical help. We were asked to clarify our match-funding, and re-submitted our application in September of that year. In December, the

WDA undertook, as an interim measure, to help us with computer and administrative backup. This they have done and, as I write, we have a full database, showing the availability of stock. This was to be followed by a Strategy Report, to be prepared by WAOS, for submission to the WDA in connection with our application. As I write, it seems to be slumbering in Cardiff.

It now transpires that yet another new organisation is to be launched: Antur Cig Cymru, a joint enterprise, comprising an elected farmer-representative, plus WDA and MLC. It has even been suggested that there is a policy-preference for a single, all-embracing enterprise of this kind. This is not a good omen. It is exactly what I feared might be initiated by WLBP. Welsh Beef is not the same thing at all as Welsh Black Beef. We would have little representation, if any, and would have little chance of establishing the niche market which our beef deserves and which would be our source of premium. A situation is now developing where fragmentation is extensive, with a considerable number of traders involved, all of them in competition with each other and having to accept prices which are not uniformly good. It calls into question any kind of control within such a market; and it leaves the field wide open for non-authentic Welsh Black beef to be passed off as the real thing.

Furthermore, the absence of specialised marketing would militate against the very thing which gives Welsh Blacks the advantage over other breeds: that it is also a suckler-breed and is best kept pure. Without a specialist marketing incentive, we might well see the very thing we have been trying to avoid: crossing, and the emergence of cross-bred suckler-cows, and even second crosses. Above all: there is no point in improving ANY stock, just for a pedigree market. Any breeders who lose sight of the commercial end product are up a blind alley.

Council are fully supportive of this principle. Of all the schemes I have done my best to promote, this is the idea which has majority support amongst ordinary members. It will take far too long to implement, but I am confident that we will succeed eventually, because our members are firmly behind it. This will probably be the last big idea I shall pursue before I retire in earnest, or at least become a Father of the Society. My own life span has encompassed the transformation of our Welsh Blacks from a suckler-cow breed with a relatively unimportant beef dimension, to a first-class beef breed with a very important suckler-cow dimension. I have seen the wider spread of the breed, which has stimulated our prices very considerably, and this is a factor which should not be underestimated.

We now need to offer stock with
(i)   stress on our 'extra dimension',
(ii) backup of objective data on health status and performance, and
(iii) evidence of special eating quality.

This special eating quality, mentioned in item (iii) is yet another reason why Welsh Black beef needs to be marketed as a separate entity. It is vital to the image of any breed, but one like ours in particular. So, we battle on with building the Welsh Black Cattle Society Beef Marketing Group. Nothing that is worth doing is ever quite finished.

I had just about concluded this autobiography when something new occurred: I was made Chairman of the WBS, and this means that, for the foreseeable future, I shall be travelling about, attending meetings and keeping up with old friends. With luck, some of my hopes and aspirations for the breed might yet come to fruition, and I shall have no excuse for not doing my utmost to improve the marketing of Welsh Black beef.

Recently, Welsh Black beef came top in a special tasting of fillet steak by 12 top London chefs.

FOOTNOTE:

There has been progress in marketing Welsh Black beef since I concluded my story. On December 12th, 2002, at the Welsh Black Beef Marketing Group AGM, when Mr. Arwyn Davies of the W.D.A. was the guest speaker, it appeared as if the seeds were sown for the beginning of a reorganisation and centralisation of our marketing efforts. We were told that 60% match-funding would be needed and were given three options to consider before the next Executive meeting, to be held on 20th January, 2003.

APPENDIX

RULES

1. The object of the Society is to maintain the purity of the Welsh Black Cattle, and promote their improvement.

2. To collect, verify, preserve, and publish in a Herd Book the Pedigrees of the said Cattle, and other useful information relating to them.

3. The Annual Subscription of Members shall be Five Shillings for persons who earn their living mainly by Farming, being Tenant Farmers or Owners of not exceeding 200 Acres of Land, and One Pound for all other Persons. Members shall pay Two Shillings and Sixpence for each Animal entered in the Herd Book; Non-Members, Five Shillings. Dead Animals, to whom Living Animals are traced, shall be entered Free to Members.

4. The affairs of the Society shall be administered by the President, Vice-Presidents, a Working Committee of Twenty-Four Members, and the Secretaries and Treasurers, to be elected at the Annual General Meeting.

6. A Sub-Committee of Four Members, with the President and Secretaries, shall determine the conditions on which entries may be made, and arrange the time, mode, and terms of issue of the Herd Book.

6. The Secretaries shall give a Certificate to the Owner of every Animal entered which shall be valid and sufficient till the next Volume of the Herd Book is published.

7. Any person dissatisfied with the decision of the Committee as to the admission or exclusion of an Animal from the Herd Book may appeal to the General Annual Meeting, whose decision shall be final.

8. All Committees may hold Meetings at such times and places as they may think fit.

9. A General Annual Meeting shall be held alternately ill North and South Wales to receive the Report of the Committees, and to Audit the Treasurers' Account: such Meeting to be fixed by the Working Committee. Extraordinary Meetings may be convened by notice being given to the Secretaries, signed by not less than Seven Members, in case of any matter requiring investigation.

10. No Rules shall be altered except at a General Annual Meeting, and two-thirds of those present at such Meeting must be in favour of the proposed alteration Notice of any such proposed alteration must be lodged with the Secretaries Twenty-One Days before the Meeting, and specified in the notice or advertisement calling the Meeting.

All information connected with the Society, may be obtained from the Secretaries, Messrs. JAMES THOMAS & SON, 9, Victoria Place, Haverfordwest.

Aberdyfi: The Past Recalled – Hugh M Lewis £6.95

You Don't Speak Welsh – Sandi Thomas £5.95

Ar Bwys y Ffald – Gwilym Jenkins £7.95

Blodeuwedd – Ogmore Batt £6.95

Black Mountains – David Barnes £6.95

Choose Life! – Phyllis Oostermeijer £5.95

Cwpan y Byd a dramâu eraill – J O Evans £4.95

Dragonrise – David Morgan Williams £4.95

The Fizzing Stone – Liz Whittaker £4.95

The Wonders of Dan yr Ogof – Sarah Symons £6.95

Aberdyfi: Past and Present – Hugh M Lewis £6.95

Dysgl Bren a Dysgl Arian – R Elwyn Hughes £9.95

Clare's Dream – J Gillman Gwynne £5.95

A Dragon To Agincourt – Malcolm Price £6.95

The Dragon Wakes – Jim Wingate £6.95

Stand Up and Sing – Beatrice Smith £4.95

For more information about the Dinas imprint contact Lefi Gruffudd at

Y Lolfa Cyf., Talybont, Ceredigion SY24 5AP
e-mail ylolfa@ylolfa.com
website www.ylolfa.com
tel. (01970) 832 304
fax 832 782
isdn 832 813